The Ultimate
GARDENING
Book

The Ultimate
GARDENING
Book

Over 1,000 inspirational ideas and practical tips to transform your garden

COLLINS & BROWN

First published in 1998 by Kiln House Books
Kiln House, 210 New Kings Road
London SW6 4NZ

Distributed in the United States by Sterling Publishing Co,
387 Park Avenue South, New York, NY 10016, USA

5 7 9 8 6 4

ISBN 1-85585-738-3

Editorial consultant: Carole McGlynn

Writers: Sharon Amos and Richard Rosenfeld
Editors: Corinne Ashgar and Katie Bent
Design Manager: Alison Lee
Designers: Sue Metcalfe-Megginson, Ruth Prentice and Alison Shackleton

Reproduction by Colour Symphony, Singapore
Printed and bound in Singapore

Contents

Your Garden:
An Introduction

There are many diverse garden styles and countless plants to choose from when planning your garden. Use this book as a source of inspiration and a guide to help you create your own individual style.

CLASSIC GARDEN STYLE
This spacious and well-tended garden (left) *combines a beautiful lawn with neat borders of shrubs and roses* (above) *for a formal effect.*

Introduction

Creating a brand new garden, or upgrading one that already exists, is an exciting task, giving you the opportunity to express your imagination to produce a garden that is all your own. But where do you start? There is a bewildering array of plants and accessories available. This book will help and inspire you to choose those for your ideal garden. It is full of ideas for many different garden styles, from the small backyard crammed full of containers to formal gardens, ponds, and desert gardens. Think about what appeals to you; the type of mood or atmosphere that you would like to create; how you will use the garden – as an area for relaxing or entertaining, as a playground for children, for growing cut flowers, herbs or vegetables, as a peaceful retreat – then think about how you can make the most of your space.

The first section of the book, 'The Contained Garden', takes an intimate look at planting schemes for courtyards, patios, and areas around the house that can be enhanced by the use of containers. Ideas are given for enlivening entrances, steps, seating areas, window boxes, and window sills – even the smallest space on a balcony or roof garden can be brought to life with a few pots full of color and scent. Areas of large gardens, such as patios, can also benefit from the addition of a few carefully placed pots or containers.

You will find ideas for planting containers through the seasons, for color themes and foliage plants, with a selection of suitable plants in the 'Gardener's Choice' pages to help you on your way.

Even in an established garden, you can use containers for special purposes: to grow herbs for the kitchen; to introduce a small water feature; for alpines and succulents, or simply as decorative details that add to the overall theme. Potted plants may be large or small-scale, and the possibilities are endless.

The second section, 'The Garden in Bloom', is a beautiful introduction to the splendors of beds and borders where flowers reign supreme. To create the maximum impact, you must plan your planting carefully. You will find advice to help you

SPRING CONTAINERS

OPPOSITE: *Yellow pansies and purple violas have been placed in a pot on the patio to add color to a late spring border.*

COLORFUL COMBINATIONS

RIGHT: *Flowers for beds and borders can be put together in stunning color combinations. Here, the red rose and purple lisianthus clash to great effect with the orange of the pot marigold.*

GREEN AND SERENE

BELOW LEFT: A gravel path leads you through this delightful formal white garden, its geometric beds bordered by low hedges of box.

HARMONY IN RED

BELOW RIGHT: This spring border of pink and red tulips is a perfect example of how to use strong colors for instant success.

plan out a bed that will work all year round. Trees and shrubs help to establish a framework within which perennials, bulbs, and annuals become star players in their own flowering season. Evergreen trees and shrubs are essential ingredients, often adding a cool relief of green to the exuberance of the floral display. Remember the effects of foliage, especially from those trees or shrubs that shed leaves of glorious colors in the fall. This section also looks at climbers and tall plants, such as scented roses and clematis, that you can use to create height at the back of the border.

Color is the key to a successful garden. You can choose from a whole spectrum of flower and foliage colors to create clever combinations that will please the eye. A hot palette of reds and oranges will produce a vibrant effect, or choose from the cooler range of blues, pinks, and purples for a calmer, more romantic feel. For maximum impact you can plan your borders along a single color scheme, but mixing colors gives you endless effects. Harmonies, such as the restful silver, blue, and white or a more vibrant yellow, orange, and red, are instantly successful. For strong visual effect try contrasts, such as purple and yellow, or pink and orange. A selection of plants from different color palettes is suggested in the final chapter of this section.

PERFECT PLANTING
LEFT: *Make the most of your available space. This small window box has been generously planted with petunias and geraniums to make an exuberant summer display that can be enjoyed both inside and outside the house.*

In the third part of the book, 'Garden Style', you will find the different elements that create the essence of the garden. The types of plants that you choose and the style in which the garden is laid out depends on how you plan to use your garden; think about whether a formal or informal effect suits you, if you enjoy eating outside, relaxing in the sunshine, escaping into a peaceful haven, or resting with the sound of water. You will find that a garden designed to fit your lifestyle will be endlessly rewarding. Think about how much time you will be able to devote to tending and maintaining the garden: a lawn, for example, needs regular tending, whereas a paved area requires less effort. The 'hard' landscaping – the paths, walls, steps, and paved areas – provides a framework; either use what already exists or add elements as required. You can add further embellishments, such as decking, arches, raised beds, and gates, to suit your chosen style.

Once your framework is in place, think about how to use your plants to best effect. Take into account the type of soil that you have, the amount of sun and shade that your garden receives, and the effect that you want to create. Plants can be used as features in their own right, guiding you through the garden to views and vistas, or creating highlights with stunning flowers and foliage. Think of how your garden will look throughout the year, not just in the summer months when it will be bursting with life. This section gives suggestions for seasonal plants, and plants that fulfil a particular need, such as climbers for walls and trellises, plants for sun and shade, and plants for year-round interest.

The final section of the book, 'Garden Themes', is a wonderful collection of inspirational ideas. To make the most of your garden, why not design it around a particular theme? Themed gardens are increasingly popular and allow you to bring a touch of your own personality and style to your outdoor space. For a flower garden, you can choose the traditional cottage style, with spires of hollyhocks and rambling roses, to add a touch of the picturesque, or, for a more formal feel, enclose neatly pruned shrub roses in low hedges of trimmed box for an elegant rose garden. Flowers can be enjoyed both in the garden and in the house: include a cut-flower garden in your planting scheme.

Water gardens have special appeal. The inclusion of water can range from a wall-mounted fountain to a formal pool or informal pond. Water has a very calming effect and is often a key feature in oriental-style gardens, together with the judicious use of gravel and pebbles. This type of dry garden can be adapted for any climate, but there are

WATER GARDEN

BELOW: An informal pond, surrounded by boulders and palm trees, brings a feeling of cool relief to a hot garden.

particular styles that suit hot, sunny sites. Desert and alpine gardens thrive in full sun: cacti and succulents will add a very unusual theme to a hot, dry garden.

If you haven't the conditions for the 'Wild West' look, but possess a shady, dappled corner instead, then why not try a woodland theme? There are many plants that add sparkles of color to even the darkest corners. Wildflowers and meadow grasses can also be used in the garden for a natural approach. You can attract the hum of bees and delicate butterflies with particular plants, adding an extra dimension to your garden.

Kitchen gardens are for those gardeners who wish to experience the delights of eating home-grown produce, and, designed with care, they can be made to look as ornamental as any flower garden. With a little forward planning and preparation, your garden can yield a continuous supply of fresh vegetables, salad crops, and fruit. Herbs are complementary to both the flower and kitchen garden. Many herbs are extremely decorative, and will benefit

ENCLOSED CALM
BELOW: *This peaceful, low-maintenance roof-top garden is enclosed by a trellis to protect against winds.*

COOL STYLE

OPPOSITE: *This individual garden uses color effectively.*

GLORIOUS YUCCA

BELOW LEFT: *Architectural plants can make key features in the garden. Yucca is ideal for hot, sunny sites.*

SUN AND SHADE

BELOW RIGHT: *This trellised wall adds a touch of welcome shade to a hot site.*

any garden whether in a traditional potager or planted in containers. Throughout each section, the 'Gardener's Choice' pages will help you to choose suitable plants to recreate a particular look. At the end of the book you will find some practical suggestions for maintaining your garden throughout the year, and a list of plants for particular situations, for quick and easy reference.

Gardening is a very rewarding pastime; you can devote as much or as little time to it as you wish and you will find that all your efforts are worthwhile. Think about how you intend to use your garden and how much time you can spend on it. Working in the garden should be a pleasure, not a chore. If you plan your garden carefully, each season will bring fresh delights. Once your garden is up and running, you can sit back and let nature take its course. Allow yourself to be inspired by the visual ideas this book contains and use them to work out a style of garden that is personal to you. With application and imagination you can create a space that will be a joy for years to come.

The Contained Garden

Around the House

Give your garden or yard a face-lift by 'decorating' it with colorful pot plants. Grow them in all kinds of containers for hanging on walls, standing on steps, and framing and highlighting special features around the house. You can even use them to create a roof garden.

EXTRA DIMENSIONS

Add a vital extra dimension to a small area near the house by packing it with layers of pot plants (left), such as universal pansies (above).

THE MINIMALIST LOOK

LEFT: *Spare, attractive architecture needs a judicious use of pots. Because the pots themselves are a feature, make sure that the most attractive – like this olive pot – are eye-catchingly placed at the front.*

THE VERSAILLES LOOK

RIGHT: *These Versailles tubs planted with standard-trained formal privet, soft, trailing evergreen ivies, and summer petunias create a stately entrance.*

THE COTTAGE LOOK

BELOW LEFT: *The best way to liven up the area by a front door opening onto the street is to pile it high with pots, so the flowers eventually hide the containers. A gorgeously scented rose frames the door.*

Entrances

It does not matter what style your home is – informal or formal, casual or stately – potted plants can immediately highlight whatever 'look' you are trying to achieve. The rule could not be simpler. With strong, disciplined architecture you need distinctive, architectural plants. Use a pair of evergreens such as bay (there are two kinds, *Laurus nobilis* or the yellow-leaved 'Aurea') or box, either side of the door. Even better, flank the approach to the entrance with two rows of evergreens, the smallest specimen at the front near the road, the tallest by the front door, imparting a theatrical sense of importance. Standard evergreens can be bought ready-shaped, or you can easily prune your own.

Cottages and country homes need a different approach; let the plants overwhelm the architecture. You need punchy, ebullient bursts of all kinds of scents and colors. Try different arrangements using everything from exotic angel's trumpets to lilies, from subtropical bougainvilleas to fuchsias, and from climbing, scrambling solanum to bright, brash pelargoniums and nasturtiums.

SUMMER STYLE
LEFT: *This exuberant, mid-summer show is achieved with pots of white marguerite daisies, petunias, lobelia, and pink lavatera.*

SPRING BULBS
OPPOSITE: *Steps make a fine alternative if you do not have space for spring bedding. These tulips are grown with pansies, a rhododendron, and a variegated hosta.*

THE ALL-GREEN THEME
BELOW: *A descending row of pots with ivy trained as a pyramid, well clipped box, and curly-leaved parsley, meets a splash of white petunias at the bottom.*

Steps

Steps, like paths, are often forgotten. But they are a great opportunity for packing in more plants, for softening hard, harsh features, and for injecting extra style. You cannot beat a rising flight of steps lined by pots to one side, giving color to a plain setting.

Evergreens are fantastic value because they brighten up the dullest steps all year. In fact they give three very good choices. You can repeat plants, using exactly the same shaped plants all the way up the steps, such as vertical, pencil thin conifers. You can try the full range of topiary shapes, everything from mini-teddy bears to pyramids. Or you can be really ambitious, and use potted evergreens to create a long, serpentlike shape winding up from the bottom. More attractive steps need only be enlivened twice a year, with pots of spring tulips, and late summer-fall performers such as fuchsias. Ferns are excellent for decorating steps in the shade.

CREATING AN ENCLOSURE

LEFT: *The best way to create a sense of privacy and build up layers of pot plants is to create some staging. Place the pots on the ground, on plinths, and even on outdoor shelving, with wooden boards supported by large, stout pots.*

TABLE SCHEMES

RIGHT: *When no one is eating at the table, use it for an extra display of pots. Shallow bowls of petunias and daisies are clustered on the table, with mixed pots on the ground.*

THE OUTDOOR LOUNGE

BELOW LEFT: *Spacious, carefully controlled seating areas need a matching background. These well-shaped evergreens blend with the restrained simplicity of the scene. Everything is laid-back and elegant.*

Seating Areas

Take the garden right up to the seating area using the most mobile form of gardening: potted plants. Surround the seats with carefully placed pots and hanging baskets to add a bright, colorful show. When the plants flag, replace them with others in bloom. The seating area will become part of the whole garden, somewhere to relax and enjoy the scenery.

Include plants with profuse flowers, good shape, and scent. Summer annuals, especially petunias, meet the first demand, with topiary meeting the second. For scent try forms of *Narcissus jonquilla* and *Hyacinthus orientalis* in the spring, followed by lilac, and the dwarf mock orange *Philadelphus microphyllus*, for midsummer. Small roses such as the crimson 'Empereur du Maroc', which grows to 4 ft (1.2 m), are also essential. This has its main flower burst in high summer. One to flower all season is the pink hybrid tea rose 'Anna Pavlova', which is slightly smaller. The key to success is that the seating areas are in warm, sheltered spaces where the scents can hang in the air.

Garden Rooms

When winter sets in, and nothing is happening outside, consider a garden room or conservatory. Here, you can keep a far wider range of plants than you thought possible, with everything from tender citrus plants, such as *Citrus* x *meyeri* 'Meyer' which likes humid conditions and gives you a year-round supply of fresh lemons, to *Jasminum polyanthum*. Tender pelargoniums enjoy the comfort and shelter and will reward you with blooms. A huge variety can be grown in different pots. You will need to provide bright sun, heating, insulation, some humidity, and shading or the plants will roast in high summer, and plenty of ventilation, even in winter, to prevent the build-up of pests and diseases, and to eliminate stagnant air.

When choosing plants for a garden room always visit a specialist nursery where the range of plants is often impressive. Take care when choosing climbers such as grapes because they can quickly take over, turning the room into a leafy jungle.

TENDER POTS

LEFT: *Garden rooms are ideal for creating collections of tender plants. There are hundreds of excellent pelargoniums, such as this red one, from the startling near-black to white.*

RELAXED COMFORT

LEFT: *The perfect balance between a sitting room and a greenhouse, neatly arranged with showy red pelargoniums. Repeat plantings such as this are enormously impressive, adding a sense of exuberance.*

REFINED ELEGANCE

RIGHT: *The ultimate garden room with marble floors, style, and space.*

Balconies and Roofs

You can create a container garden right in the heart of the city, using your balcony or roof space. The main decision is whether the aerial garden is to be self-enclosed, screening out the city, or part of the total scene. You can plant a floral haven or you might prefer to use the space for a bright, culinary garden with strawberries and tomatoes, or garlic, basil, and rocket. As with any small garden space, the key to the right look is choosing one particular style and sticking to it. But creating a garden paradise in the air is not easy, at least if you do it yourself. Always call in the experts as drainage, weight, and wind all pose problems. However, once these obstacles are overcome, you can have trees, and shrubs, as well as perennials, herbs, and annuals planted all around the edges of your outdoor space.

SMART DETAIL

ABOVE: Simplicity is the key to making a small garden work. Here, the white rail of the balcony is laced with a climber, while white roses in a large planter are offset by catmint.

NEW YORK VIEWS

RIGHT: A good example of how practical needs can be aesthetically pleasing. Low-growing plants emphasize the views; tall plants would be flayed by the winds.

Window Boxes and Sills

Window boxes are highly versatile. You can use them for seasonal bedding with spring daffodils, summer annuals, and fall and winter evergreens. You can color-coordinate your schemes for hothouse reds or pale pastels or you can concentrate on scent. When planting, remember that the plants will be visible from both inside and outside the window. Window boxes are also good at giving part of the building's exterior a quick make-over. Tumbling, trailing ivies come with all kinds of leaf shape, from the bird's foot to the curly-edged, to the diamond-, fan-, and heart-shaped. The key to success, as with all containers, is firm fixings and excellent drainage. Old tins, used as containers, need plenty of drainage holes, and all need crocks or polystyrene chips placed at the bottom before the addition of soil.

A SPRING TROUGH

RIGHT: *A mix of primulas, cineraria, and anemones. You can replace the spring display with herbs in summer.*

A TOUCH OF THE BLUES

LEFT: *You can use almost anything as a container, like these tins with drainage holes drilled into the back.*

ELEGANT EXTRAS

OPPOSITE: *Smart period buildings need smart troughs. This is richly planted with pelargoniums.*

31

POWERFUL PETUNIAS

ABOVE: *There is now a huge color range of petunias, and some are wonderfully vibrant. The dark reds and blues, and paler colors are the easiest to use. Keep deadheading them all season for a continuous supply of flowers.*

SUMMER EXCESS

RIGHT: *With an informal window box, the fuller the planting the better. Here, pelargoniums, petunias, lobelia, and helichrysum have been packed tightly together for maximum effect. Make sure that window boxes are regularly watered, which in high temperatures can mean twice a day. Note how the dwarf conifer and hebe give a permanent evergreen structure.*

Hanging Baskets

The best hanging baskets are part of a color-packed scheme. They reach the parts that climbers never quite reach, and which the window box trailers keep on missing. Hanging baskets are commonly planted out in the summer months, when their exuberant display of flowers and foliage disguise the container beneath. They need not be tastefully gentle; they can create a riot of color with flashes of yellows, reds, blues, and whites. Walk around the garden, pinpointing suitable places; and that includes branches, beams, arches, and metal structures. You will be surprised how many eye-catchers you might have room for. Try to avoid hanging baskets in isolation, unrelated to anything else. Always make sure that your baskets sit happily within the overall scheme.

CREATING NEW BASKETS

ABOVE LEFT: *Newly planted baskets take time before they take off. It is always worth having a special place to hang and keep an eye on them, pinching out plants to make them bushier, before putting them in their final position.*

THE FINAL TOUCH

OPPOSITE: *This gazebo has been finished with a pink and white hanging basket. It guarantees a splash of color at every level.*

BASKETS IN THEIR PRIME

LEFT: *This wonderful display includes fuchsias, petunias, and lobelias. The plants will only look this good with regular watering and feeding. Attaching the basket to a pulley means it can easily be lowered for a good evening drink, minimizing the degree of evaporation. Add a slow-release fertilizer to the compost when planting.*

35

On a practical level, note that freshly watered baskets dramatically increase in weight. What was light and easy to handle suddenly becomes immensely heavy, so the fittings need to be extremely strong and sturdy. Also avoid hanging the baskets in windy places where they can get blown around and check that there is no danger of anyone walking into them. Watering can be made easier by using a pulley system for lowering the basket, or by using a ready-made spray attached to a pipe or cane. Just raise it up into the center of the plants and water accordingly.

PINK AND WHITE

LEFT: *A summer scheme with diascias, fuchsia, verbena, busy Lizzies, and the excellent yellow* Bidens ferulifolia.

GREEN AND YELLOW

RIGHT: *These gentle shades tone well with the subtle color of the stone building.*

Planting a hanging basket

Plants in a hanging basket will flourish if they are properly planted and maintained. You need a firm base or holder (such as an empty pot or bucket), damp sphagnum moss, polythene, granules of slow-release fertilizer, water-retaining crystals, and relatively light, soil-less compost. Select your plants carefully, ensuring that you include something to add height in the center. The final rule is to always take your time.

1 *Firmly balance the basket on an empty pot, and then pack it with handfuls of damp sphagnum moss.*

2 *Line the sphagnum moss with polythene. Trim it flush to the top, and cut slits all round every 3 in (7.5 cm).*

3 *Insert the trailing plants first. Working up from the bottom, push them through the holes from the inside.*

4 *Use the tallest vertical plant top center, with trailers around. The soil surface should be 1 in (2.5 cm) below the rim.*

STYLISH SHELVES

ABOVE: *This simple, highly effective purpose-made scheme is no more than a blue shelf with holes for the pots, mounted on strong brackets. It gains great impact by ordered repeat planting using gorgeous, red pelargoniums.*

ANNUALS ARE BEST

LEFT: *Since wall pots hold half the amount of compost of an ordinary pot, stick to bedding and shallow-rooted plants such as these lovely purple petunias.*

Wall Pots

Take a lesson from the small courtyard, Greek-island gardens. When planting, utilize every space, and that includes bare walls. Treat them as a kind of vertical flower bed. Attach pots to the surfaces, arranging them in rows, pots with trailing orange nasturtiums, with lipstick-pink pelargoniums, with deep blue verbenas, and *Bidens ferulifolia* with sprays of bright yellow, daisylike flowers. You can use anything from terracotta pots to painted containers, to ornamental tins, even a collection of watering cans. Equally important, wall pots are a good way of softening severe architectural features, and brings the garden to an end much more gently than a harsh, bare wall. Decorating an end wall with plants means that you blur and upgrade the boundary. It is a clever trick that is well worth copying.

MERGING COLORS

ABOVE: *Instead of going for the vibrant approach with contrasting bright colored flowers, try using soft blues and purples to create a gentler ambience.*

CREATING SPRAYS

LEFT: *It is easy to concentrate on color and forget about shape, but a wonderful spray of flowers opening from a tight conelike container can be a magical feature. Here, the star plants are felicias and swan river daisies.*

39

Helichrysum petiolare

White and blue trailing lobelia with *Convolvulus sabatius*.

Lobelia erinus 'Fountain Select'

Fuchsia 'Jack Shahan'

Trailing Plants

When choosing plants for wall pots and hanging baskets, always include some excellent trailers. They swamp and cover the container with growth, giving a sense of luxury, and they blur the gaps between plants. The range of subjects is huge, from those with textured foliage to great masses of summery flowers.

Felicia amelloides

Close-up on Containers

There is now a terrific range of pots, and with the increasing variety of plants available, getting the right style pot for the right mix of plants can be tricky. The quickest way to success is to borrow or adapt some of the ideas shown on the following pages.

CREATIVE CONTAINERS

A careful grouping of containers enhances any garden (left); shapely plants and a clever use of color, such as this flash of orange (above), *make stunning focal points.*

Choosing Containers

Containers come in all shapes and sizes, as well as materials. Since many can be quite expensive, it is worth studying what is on offer before making a final choice. The best in terracotta, Italian-style swagged pots with fabulous. elaborate decorations, are wonderful but can be expensive. The bottom-of-the-range pots can be plain and simple, but a pot of paint will transform them. Shiny metal containers make a smart surprise, and most need painting with a preservative to keep rust at bay. Wooden containers need anti-rot treatment, and are perfect as large containers for fig trees, or camellias which have to be grown in acid soil. Stone containers always look good, but they are heavy and expensive. Plastic containers are inexpensive and ideal for raising cuttings.

A standard pot with violas

'Long Toms'

Terracotta window boxes

Pink mimulus in a bowl

A trio of terracotta pots in various shapes

Terracotta seed pan

THE CONTAINER GARDEN

ABOVE: *This effusive cascade is an excellent example of how good a massive collection of plants can look. Yellow-leaved hops and delicate sweet peas punctuate the mass of green and complement the rich terracotta of the pots.*

Lattice seed pan

Don't forget the range of hanging baskets, mangers, and wall pots that are also available. A combination of different sizes, styles, and heights is very effective. You can also make your own containers. You can easily adapt old boots and buckets, baths and sinks, making them into novelty containers. With the first two, make sure that you give them plenty of drainage holes. With the second two, you need to get your hands dirty, covering them with hypertufa. Clean and dry the container, then score the surface with a screwdriver or chisel. Next add a smooth covering of hypertufa to the outer surface and well inside the inner rim. Plant up when dry.

A SUMMER HANGING BASKET

ABOVE: The recipe for this bright mix is bronze-leafed tradescantia, with pink and white petunias.

Aluminum manger

Lead-style fiberglass urn

Lattice-work stone basket

Versailles tub (untreated)

Metal filigree basket

OLD-STYLE LEAD PLANTERS

ABOVE: Containers such as this need highly ambitious planting schemes. This imaginative all-green theme has plenty of size and bulk, and has been created using unusual species of plectranthus, *with a colorful array of foliage plants.*

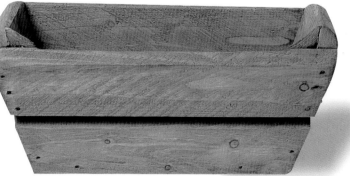

Wooden window box

Peachstone trough

Fiberglass window box

MARGUERITES

LEFT: *The great advantage of growing marguerite daisies is that they have a long flowering period, attractive, finely shaped leaves, and can either be used alone, as here, or to brighten up a group of softer colors.*

PETUNIAS

RIGHT: *Even the most effective, cleverest pot arrangements gain hugely from a stylish, symmetrical placing. These pots, elegantly framing the grandiose, ornamental French windows have a pink and white theme. They are planted with double and single petunias, pelargoniums, and white alyssum.*

OXALIS

BELOW: *Red-leafed oxalis makes a novel choice for a pot, but here gives a marvellous show of pink and maroon.*

Effective Simplicity

It is relatively easy to create a bright mix of flowers for a dramatic display. It takes a little more thought and planning to achieve elegant simplicity using one single species per pot. The results can be very effective. The rule is either to choose a plant with an eye-catching shape, or one with a mass of flowers.

Plants that belong to the first category include the South African honey bush, one of the most architectural plants for the garden. It grows to 4 ft (1.2 m) in a pot, but needs to be brought indoors over winter. Japanese maples, especially the *Acer palmatum* species such as 'Bloodgood', have a bonsai-style curvy shape and fall color, and grow to 5–8 ft (1.5–2.5 m). The black bamboo and dwarf grasses, hostas and yuccas should all be on your shopping list. But the cordylines are the most effective, especially the purple, strap-leaved *C. australis*. Use topiarized box for the Italian look. Try a single stem with a series of balls, the largest at the bottom, the smallest right at the top.

For flower power the range is even greater. Agapanthus, cosmos, felicia, fuchsias with thick, rust-red stems, hydrangeas, gorgeous bright red salvias, and sweet peas, all make vivid plantings. The season kicks off with tulips. Always stick to one variety per pot, or the color scheme loses impact. Floppy verbenas, such as the pink 'Sissinghurst', can be trained up a frame of canes that really shows off their colors. Lilies are a must for the summer, especially the easily grown, highly scented, white *Lilium regale*. And if you need something extra, try the annual climber *Rhodochiton atrosanguineus*. It has purple, bell-shaped summer flowers with a splendid protruding black 'clapper', and grows to 6 ft (1.8 m) – a real eye-catcher.

Viola 'Molly Sanderson'

Clipped box in a ribbed pot

BRIGHT AND SIMPLE

LEFT: *Tulips are so beautiful that you do not need to use highly ornamental pots – a simple square container is more than adequate.*

MASSED REDS

RIGHT: *Pelargoniums offer a range of colors but nothing beats classic red. They are always highly impressive when in full flower.*

SUNNY SIMPLICITY

LEFT: *Gardens need surprises, a clever change of emphasis, or something that brings them alive, such as this cheerful trio of sunflowers in pots.*

BRIGHT YELLOWS

BELOW: *Potted marigolds, here* Calendula 'Lemon Beauty', *make a bold, bushy group. Individual pots are very good at filling any gaps that appear in the border.*

53

Creating Impact

Creating impact is one thing, doing it well is another. Visit the very best gardens for inspiration, see how they do things, use their best ideas, then inject some of your own. Forget all about taste and fashion. You could use color-graded schemes, starting off with soft hues and building up to hot reds in the center, then tapering away into pale pinks and grays. Alternatively, there is no reason at all why you can not add a touch of Van Gogh to your garden, using a riot of clashing reds and yellows. The key point is that impact is not an individual, separate entity. It is the effect of something reacting with or against something else. Impact is created by color or shape. In a new, bare garden that means spending as much time on the background as on creating the colorful mix of 'fireworks'.

Containers are perfect for mixing a variety of plants, colors, textures, and shapes; plant them individually then mass them together to create a floral explosion. Don't forget your walls and empty spaces; hanging baskets add an extra dimension.

Petunia

IMPACT BY NUMBERS

LEFT: *The success of this simple scheme has two bases. One is the bold use of strong reds and pinks against a white background, the other is the grouping of bushy plants using hanging baskets to create aerial mounds.*

INJECTING PROFUSION

RIGHT: *If you want to give a courtyard impact, pack it with color. Everything here is growing in containers. The scheme includes ageratum, petunias, cosmos, pelargoniums, lobelia, and plenty of nicotiana.*

QUICK CONTRASTS

LEFT: *To decide where a new plant will have most impact, walk round the garden with it, seeing where it stands out. This red hydrangea makes a nice contrast against a wall of cool green.*

IMPACT WITH HANGING BASKETS

RIGHT: *If your front door needs a lift, give it a flash of yellow* Bidens ferulifolia. *The impact is always sensational. The red begonia on the step, and the pink roses, neatly fill out the scene.*

SPRING YELLOWS

BELOW LEFT: *Yellows always look dramatic against dark backgrounds. This clever, tiered spring group includes auriculas at the front, with daffodils and wallflowers, dicentra in the center, and forget-me-nots to the sides.*

Creating impact with color requires plants with a big display. One plant that has got what it takes is the tender crimson bottlebrush. It pumps out a great mass of bright red cylindrical flowers, on the end of long stems, and keeps performing through early summer. It looks startling with yellow nasturtiums. Another strong summer yellow is *Lilium* 'Citronella' which sends flowers up to 5 ft (1.5 m), looking like tropical butterflies. Use them as the pinnacle for a summer scheme with blue teasels, white marguerites, and the gray *Helichrysum petiolare*. For a no-nonsense fall scarlet try *Fuchsia* 'Riccartonii' which stands out when most other plants have faded, and for the really exotic, use South American summer cannas and late summer dahlias.

Plants with shapely impact need space around them to stand out. Do not engulf them in a blur of colors. One of the best is *Yucca recurvifolia*, which has a strong rosette of bent, swordlike leaves, and thrusts up a 6 ft (1.8 m) stem

packed with scores of white flowers. It is a great dramatic event. If you need more height, then *Verbascum bombyciferum* grows to 8 ft (2.5 m), with wonderful fleshy leaves and great spires with yellow flowers. But to be really outrageous you need the cardoon, *Cynara cardunculus*, which is just like a giant thistle, 5 ft (1.5 m), with blue flowers. The taller mahonias, such as *Mahonia* x *media* 'Buckland', are essential for winter interest. They have a statuesque presence, shiny green leaves, and scented yellow flowers. Judicious pruning imposes shape on the shapeless. For other strong shapes use agaves, banana trees, cordylines, and olive trees. All guarantee you success and a real impact.

BIG POTS FOR BIG DISPLAYS
LEFT: This enormous display mixes the spiky leaves of a cordyline with red salvias, a yellow abutilon, gold bidens, and yellow marguerites.

VERTICAL SPEARS
BELOW: Astelia nervosa, *from New Zealand, is a clump-forming perennial.*

THE MEXICAN TOUCH
LEFT: Agave americana 'Marginata', from Mexico, has such an oustanding shape it stands out in most situations.

FORMAL SYMMETRY
RIGHT: This bright combination of plants and colors is given extra drama and impact by the inclusion of the vivid blue chair.

SPIKED SPLENDOR
LEFT: Leymus arenarius *is ideal for pots because in the border it can spread and spread. It is a terrific plant, with stiff, blue-green foliage.* Carex *is to either side.*

THE CURTAIN EFFECT
RIGHT: *Plants such as this trailing catmint are just what you need with a brand new urn. If its newness looks out of place, half-hide it under a curtain of leaves.*

SMART DETAIL
BELOW: *Every garden need its quiet moment. This* Pelargonium *'Vancouver Centennial' is a miniature amongst some giants.*

Foliage for Containers

Any garden, with or without pots, needs to break away from the idea that everything is geared toward flowers. Yes, they count. Yes, they can lift the spirits. But so does foliage. There is a great variety of shapes and tints and textures. The invaluable evergreens last all year.

The enormous range of foliage shapes and textures falls into three categories: one for thrusting, vertical foliage; one for tiers and mounds; and one for trailers. The first is the most exciting, and includes bamboos and grasses. *Arundinaria falconeri* grows to 7 ft (2.1 m), and has thin, swishing stems. For a grass try *Arundo donax* which has 10 ft (3 m) high jungly stems. Alternatively there are pencil-thin conifers, which can be used to frame a scene. *Juniperus communis* 'Compressa' grows just 2ft 8in (80 cm, being 18 in (45 cm) wide.

For a tiered effect try *Cornus controversa*, sometimes called the wedding cake tree. For a high yellow mound you need one of the conifers, ideally *Chamaecyparis pisifera* 'Filifera Aurea', and for a marvellous, monster look-alike there is *Cedrus deodara* 'Gold Mound'. It needs a big tub but has wonderful shaggy 'arms'. In shady areas try hostas. They actually look incredibly smart in pots, the compost topped by pebbles. For trailing plants you cannot beat ivies.

FIVE-COLORED CLIMBER
ABOVE: Actinidia kolomikta *has purple-tinted new foliage, turning green with a white then pink tip. In fall it is red.*

OVAL SHAPES
ABOVE: Spiraea, hosta, and sage offer a range of size and texture.

Clover (*Oxalis triangularis* 'Cupido')

Purple sage
(*Salvia officinalis* 'Purpurascens')

Fuchsia 'Thalia'

Anthriscus sylvestris
'Moonlit Night'

PERFECT PATIO

RIGHT: *An array of neatly juxtaposed foliage plants, featuring a variegated hosta, fine-leafed fern, and a smooth, neatly clipped ball of Osmanthus x burkwoodii.*

Deadnettle
(*Lamium maculatum*)

Ivy (*Hedera helix* 'White Knight')

Ivy (*Hedera helix* 'Adam')

63

Evergreens

Every garden needs great clusters of evergreens, plants that will keep performing all year, summer and winter, in frost, drought, and snow.

When gardeners speak of color, they rarely mean green, but green is an excellent color with a variety of hues from bright green, olive green, blue-green to dark green. This constant show helps provide the garden with backbone, a permanent structure that divides the garden, creating areas where you can place the colors.

When it comes to individual eye-catchers, the choice is huge. *Choisya ternata* forms a glossy mound with spring-scented flowers. *Euphorbia rigida* makes a marvellous array of brown stems, with fleshy green leaves topped by yellow in early summer. *Euonymus fortunei* 'Silver Queen' makes a bright variegated shrub. Conifers provide all kinds of shapes with verticals, ovals, horizontals, and even tall, thin spires. *Garrya elliptica* 'James Roof', with its mid-winter catkins, provides the best winter displays.

BOX BALLS AND DECKING

ABOVE: The best, all-purpose box for topiary is Buxus sempervirens. *It can be pruned into cones, spirals, balls, large globes, and standards.*

THE IVY LEAGUE

LEFT: Ivies are woefully underrated. They easily reach those parts other plants cannot get to, covering any bare gaps on walls. They can be pruned and shaped at will from spring to fall.

STAGGERING HEIGHTS

FAR LEFT: A well staged show with a build-up in height using clipped box and conifer, offset by white marguerites.

FRAMED BY BOX

RIGHT: The area is defined by evergreens, within which are the feature plants. These include a fruiting citrus with cacti to add an extra layer of interest.

ROOSTING CHICKENS

ABOVE: A smart, symmetrical grouping of four birds, with a variegated ivy dove in the middle. Box and yew shapes need two trimmings a year, in spring and fall, to keep the shape and maintain a dense covering of leaves. Avoid tight-angled, intricate shapes. With small-leaved ivy you can create slightly better defined figures.

Trained Shapes

Once you start thinking shapes, you are hooked. Basically there are two traditions, the Japanese and the Western. The former is an ideal way to give round shrubs good shape. It even extends to trees. Pruning branches is a good way of making sure that a specimen does not obstruct a view, but filters it to the rest of the garden. At its most effective it results in cloud pruning, which means you can reduce a Leyland cypress to five or six long bare stems, with balls of green on top. More traditionally a Portugal laurel can be converted into a giant mushroom, with a bare stem and a wide head of foliage.

But the two most popular plants for topiary are box and yew, both excellent for creating balls, boxes, pyramids, spirals, and even animals. You can buy template shapes (open 3-D frames) from garden centers, training soft growth through and over. Also, try pruning by eye. Take a young box cutting and tweak it into shape, using stiff wire to which you tie it. A long stem becomes a neck, the middle the body, and so on. Or grow the box into a decent-sized shrub and then start shaping.

ABSTRACT THEMES

RIGHT: Topiary is about having fun. Traditional shapes such as this spiral are hugely impressive, but you can easily invent your own.

Training an ivy pyramid

This is a very simple task. All you need are two or three small-leaved ivies, a 9-in (23-cm) pot or one that is slightly larger, and a 2 ft (60 cm) high frame, or six canes, and garden wire. It will take a few weeks for the shoots to cover the frame. Constant pinching out during the growing season will speed things up.

1 *Plant the ivy, then unravel the stems. Next set up the frame, firmly fixing it in place. Use garden wire to create a criss-cross network.*

2 *Gently thread and weave the long ivy shoots between the network of wires, so that they cover as much of the shape as possible. Evenly space them out.*

The fully grown pyramid

Colorful Containers

Color schemes for containers work best when the colors match the style of container. Strong powerful pots need strong powerful colors, just as elegantly simple ones work well with gentler hues. The most important point though, is to avoid anything approaching a cacophony of colors that beg to be kept apart. As with flower arranging, select a dominant color and work around it.

The positioning of the colors is equally important. Do not lose the effect of a gorgeous dark blue flower by positioning it against a dark background. Some of the blue salvias, especially *Salvia patens*, are so vivid and rich that they desperately need a bright background to stand out. That is even truer of the deep dark wine reds, such as *Cosmos atrosanguineus*. Conversely, check that whites, yellows, and oranges are not lost against matching backgrounds. The white *Tulipa* 'Triumphator' is one of the most exquisite of all tulips, and should be grown separately, rather than in a white garden, where its appeal would be promptly diminished against a background of silvers and grays. It is also vital to note the extent to which colors create different moods; cool white lilies are restful, whilst reds and oranges are vibrant and hot.

CLASSIC SIMPLICITY

ABOVE: *An ornamental, classic style urn set on a plinth, with a fine show of red and yellow tulips. Note how they flare out against the dark, bare background, and how the vertical stems do not detract from the shape of the urn.*

A STUDY IN ORANGE

OPPOSITE: *The best way to brighten a corner is with a strong flash of orange. Patio chrysanthemums are a good choice for small pots, maintaining a shapely balance.*

Tazetta narcissus
(*Narcissus tazetta*)

Hot Reds

There are two important points to note about using hot reds. The first is that they are excellent eye-catchers; the second is that they need not be screamingly violent, brash and shocking. Reds come in all shades from the bright scarlet and crimson, to the deep, dark reds which verge on black. And because they stand out so well, you rarely need companion colors. In fact, as these photographs show, the best companions are invariably extra groupings and layers of red.

Hot strong colors do have one extra, vital use. If you want to foreshorten a view in the garden, then end it with a dark color. It makes the furthest point seem much stronger and far more solid. In the same way if you want to make a shortish view appear longer, end it with paler colors. They do not grab the eye in the same determined way, and let the view quietly peter out instead.

Fuchsia 'Thalia'

Verbena x *hybrida*

Pelargonium

RED ON WHITE

TOP LEFT: *A dashing horizontal spread of red pelargoniums.*

HOT EXOTICS

BELOW LEFT: *A lively display with crocosmias,* Canna *'King Humbert' and 'Wyoming', with* Dahlia *'Grenadier', 'The Fairy', and 'David Howard'.*

RISING REDS

RIGHT: *A cleverly engineered show with neat, wooden containers of nasturtiums, gerberas, cannas, and* Lotus berthelotii.

Perfect Pinks

Pinks come in two kinds – the bright, lipstick shocker, and the quiet one, gently fading. Make sure you know exactly which kind you are getting. When looking for companion colors, grays are always successful, as are pale blues, and the softer lilacs and mauves. And when looking for the right type of pot, faded terracotta makes a very good match. It is also worth noting that many flower buds, especially of roses, have rich pink coloring before opening to darker shades.

BASKETS FOR SUBTLETY

ABOVE: While many hanging baskets aim to explode pockets of color, it is worth noting that many are equally satisfying when trying to calm things down. This mix of busy Lizzies, pansies, and dianthus makes a gentle blend.

Petunia

Penstemon 'Garnet'

Pansy (*Viola*)

Tulips (*Tulipa*)

WINTER CHRISTMAS ROSES

RIGHT: *A good display of pink winter flowers using hellebores, hyacinths, and polyanthus.*

Verbena bonariensis

Dittany (*Origanum laevigatum*)

Scaevola aemula

DEEP PINK WINDOW SCHEME

LEFT: *This summer show includes verbena, oxalis, and pelargoniums.*

73

BLUES AND GRAYS

LEFT: *A twin-theme hanging basket, relying solely on blue-faced pansies and small-leaved gray helichrysum.*

POTTED LACECAPS

RIGHT: *A gorgeous gentle mix of blue lacecap hydrangeas with a mound of lobelia.*

BLUE AGAINST BLUE

BELOW LEFT: *An ornamental metal seat makes an excellent stage, holding up pots of petunias, helichrysums, and the blue-green, sword-shaped leaves of* Astelia nervosa *'Silver Spear', all seen against a blue-painted trellis.*

Cool Blues

Blue is an interesting color – it appears to get richer and darker for a brief spell in the early evening. That is because the eye is more sensitive to blue at dusk, in the half light, when it gains in intensity because the early evening blue light enhances the blue of the flowers.

Fortunately blue is also extremely sociable. It mixes well with most other colors, the paler shades with grays and whites, the darker ones with green. There is a good number of blue plants, from the eryngiums to hyacinths.

ELEGANT BLUES

RIGHT: *A highly effective posy of anemones, forget-me-nots, and comfrey.*

Fresh White

Amid the hustle and bustle of the modern world, it is wonderful to have a tranquil area that is easy on the eye and easy on the soul. The all-white planting has long been a favorite. White flowers have an elegant simplicity that is the envy of their more colorful counterparts. What could be easier than to bring this elegance to your garden using pots – either a single container or a whole series?

White also mixes well with all other colors, and with silver and grays it makes a good link between colors that would clash in close proximity. Placing white plants in a corner of a colorful garden instantly transforms that area into a restful haven for you to enjoy. When combined with evergreens, the effect is fresh and clean.

WHITES WITH STYLE

OPPOSITE: *The mix of Easter lilies and clipped box lifts this dark corner of a garden.*

SPIRAL OF WHITES

ABOVE LEFT: *This wirework plant holder creates a focal point in a small garden. It contains busy Lizzies, cosmos, pelargoniums, and hydrangeas.*

SIMPLE ELEGANCE

LEFT: Clematis cartmanii *is a dwarf evergreen hybrid from New Zealand that flowers in late spring. It makes a graceful white pot plant.*

Seasonal Effects

Potted plants make a terrific contribution right through the year, adding scent and color, even in winter. Here is a lively look at the best plants for each season, with everything from tulips and cyclamen to skimmia and wonderful Japanese acers.

SUMMER PLANTING

This profusion of flowers and gray foliage has been grouped together for maximum summer impact (left). Pink mophead hydrangeas add a glorious splash of color (above).

Spring

Bulbs are ideal for growing in containers to give a burst of color and scent after the winter, and there is a fabulous range available. Daffodils come in apricot, lemon, orange, pink, white, and yellow. *Narcissus triandrus* has a startling flower more like a fuchsia's; 'Bartley' has a long thin pronounced trumpet; and *N. poeticus var. recurvus* is the most beautiful white oval with a central orange eye. Some even begin flowering at the end of winter, such as 'February Gold'. For strong sweet scent go for the jonquils and the tazettas which need warm, dry sheltered conditions; the scented paperwhites make excellent indoor plants.

Also try crocuses, especially those with gorgeous feathered markings or tints on the outside such as 'Ladykiller', which is purple outside and white within. The orange flower-topped *Fritillaria imperialis* is always striking in big tubs.

SPRING CHEER

ABOVE: *These delicate spring violas bring a touch of cheer to a quiet corner of the garden.*

INDOOR SCENT

RIGHT: *The advantage of growing these white 'L'Innocence' hyacinths in a basket is that you can easily bring them indoors in bad weather to fill a room with scent.*

CLASSIC COMBINATIONS

OPPOSITE: *Red and white tulips with red wallflowers and purple pansies. With all bulbs it is vitally important that you let the foliage die down naturally; it stores up energy for next year's display.*

The maroon and yellow *Fritillaria michailovskyi* needs sharp drainage, easily created in pots. The same applies to most Juno irises. The easiest to grow are the lilac *Iris cycloglossa* and *I. magnifica*, and white to lemon *I. bucharica*, which is the pick of the bunch. Pots also shield them from slugs. Other excellent irises are the reticulatas and xiphiums, many with exquisite leaf markings. Also grow hyacinths and tulips, and the erythroniums, with their gently beautiful flowers.

Primrose
(*Polyanthus*)

BOLD JUXTAPOSITIONS

LEFT: *Start the new season with a strong, bold combination of colors such as these yellow daffodils growing with purple-blue polyanthus.*

THE MINIATURE GARDEN

RIGHT: *To fill a space by the front door, create a small-scale garden using miniature bulbs. Dwarf blue irises, low-growing daffodils, and polyanthus make a clever trio. Gravel topping has been used to highlight the stems and flowers.*

A perfect demonstration of the wide range of tulip types and colors.

Dutch tulips

Rembrandt tulip

Tulipa 'Fancy Frills'

Tulipa 'Menton'

Spring Tulips

It does not matter what color scheme you choose, tulips will provide it – soft pinks, gentle blues, hot reds, and near blacks. They generally flower in mid- and late spring, and are best dug up after the foliage has faded. Store them in a dry, warm place for planting out in early winter. If planted too early they can shoot prematurely, and get zapped by frost. The sturdier *T. greigii* and *T. kaufmanniana* hybrids can be left outside all year.

THE INFORMAL LOOK

LEFT: A soft-colored, midsummer mix of dark-eyed petunias, yellow-faced pansies, cineraria, and Argyranthemum *'Mary Wootton'.*

HIGH FORMALITY

RIGHT: Urns on plinths make the ultimate focal point. This fulsome planting involves a spread of Helichrysum petiolare, *trailing blue lobelia, petunias, and pelargoniums.*

CLIMBERS

BELOW: Where there is limited space in the garden for climbers, try propelling them out of pots. Old-fashioned sweet peas have a sensational scent and you can grow them up a wigwam of canes.

Summer

The summer show is the big one. The range of colors and shapes is huge. You can have anything from snappy hothouse colors to yellows and blues, white with black, and even a collection of jungly, floppy-leaved plants.

Lilies are fabulous summer plants. There are basically four different flower shapes – trumpets, funnels, bowls, and swept-back turkscap. Mix them up, the flower stems at different heights, including some with a very strong scent, such as the gorgeous white *Lilium longiflorum*. Colors range from the near black-purplish-red to whites speckled with maroon.

For quirky color surprises try ornamental kale with its bright center surrounded by a ruff of vivid green. But for the really startling look try the tender *Gloriosa superba* 'Rothschildiana'. It has

bright red and yellow flowers, about 5 ft (1.5 m) high above ground, and looks far too exotic for most gardens. If given a minimum winter temperature of 46°F (8°C), you will not have any problems. Stand it outside over summer. Colorful hardy geraniums are easier; they flower well all summer long.

Patio rose
(*Rosa* 'De Meaux')

OPEN ELEGANCE

LEFT: *This stylish scene works, thanks to a repeat planting of standard trained box, with scented pink patio and climbing roses, and criss-cross ironwork patterning.*

TENDER PELARGONIUMS

BELOW: *To keep your pelargoniums all year long, grow them in pots and bring them indoors in winter. Frosts and cold wet soil are lethal.*

A BALL-TOPPED MANGER
LEFT: *A clever use of bright marigolds, above a mass of variegated catmint, lobelia, and petunias.*

RISING HEIGHTS
RIGHT: *The low-level planting means no bare gaps are to be seen in this ebullient show of roses, bougainvillea, kalanchoe, and gray helichrysums.*

WHITE AND GRAY
BELOW: *This cool composition in a single pot features the wonderfully architectural* Melianthus major, *with ferny-leaved artemisia, white marguerites, and* Malva sylvestris *'Primley Blue'.*

For pot plants with interesting shapes, standards are essential. This involves reducing a plant to one vertical stem, with all the flowering taking place high up, often in a great ball of growth. The 6 ft (1.8 m) high South American brugmansias have long, theatrical, trumpet-shaped flowers. The scented yellow *Brugmansia* x *candida* 'Grand Marnier' is one of the best. Bring it indoors over winter. Standard fuchsias or marguerites are equally attractive, and can be used in pairs to frame seats and statues. And if you want something bizarrely engaging, grow one lettuce per pot. Instead of picking them, let them go to seed; they will send up long, thin, twisty stems. For the ultimate in chic, though, grow succulents and cacti. Colors range from shiny purple-blacks to olive-gray, and shapes from tiny balls to obelisks for the Wild West look.

Orange chrysanthemums in matching terracotta pots.

Browallia speciosa

Osteospermum 'Pink Whirls'

Pot marigolds (*Calendula officinalis*)

Busy Lizzie (*Impatiens* 'Accent Salmon')

Summer Bedding

Set out special summer schemes in block colors, or in patterns, restrained or exuberant, formal or informal. The bigger the better; the look is up to you. There is a wide range of plants to choose from, using annuals and perennials, in a range of colors, muted and bold.

Fall

Fall colors might be associated with great trees in giant landscape parks, but there is no reason at all why they cannot be locked up in relatively small containers to bring color to a small garden when the last flush of summer flowers are fading. For beautiful foliage, Japanese acers are the best subjects, not being too tall, generally reaching 5 ft (1.5 m) in pots. The leaves of the beautiful wild rose *R. virginiana*, turn an incredible beetroot-red when the cold comes, ending up yellow-orange. As for shrubs, *Cotoneaster horizontalis* is covered with red berries, while *Callicarpa bodinieri* 'Profusion' has berries that are shiny and lilac that will bring a dose of cheer into the garden. Chrysanthemums and asters provide a colorful spectrum of late flowers.

Chrysanthemum

GLORIOUS COLOR

LEFT: *Add a rich dimension to the fall garden using colorful foliage and late-flowering perennials. This vibrant acer makes a wonderfully bright contribution to the fall landscape, and proves that pots have as much of a place in the garden late in the year as they do in the earlier months.*

WINTER BASKET
LEFT: Foliage offers interest in a winter hanging basket.

Winter

The range of winter plants may be small, but the ones that do perform at this time of year always catch the eye. There are some very good bedding plants, such as winter pansies, but best of all are the bulbs. *Crocus tommasinianus* opens at the first hint of warmth, offering purple with 'Barr's Purple', and white with *C. albus*. A container is a good place to grow them, as in the garden they are ferocious spreaders. Also try *Cyclamen coum* which is available in white, pinks and red, the yellow winter aconite, snowdrops, especially the sturdy, white *Galanthus* 'S. Arnott', and the blue winter iris, *Iris histrioides*. All can be planted alone, or around the stems of standard shrubs such as holly, or the corkscrew hazel, *Corylus avellana* 'Contorta'.

CROCUSES
LEFT: This trio of pots shows what a good display early crocuses offer. Two particularly good peformers are the lilac Crocus laevigatus *'Fontenayi' and the lilac* C. tommasinianus.

HOLLY AND IVY
RIGHT: A neatly styled standard holly towers over white cyclamen and variegated ivy by a doorway. The cyclamen can be replaced by spring and, later, summer bedding.

SEASONAL CONTAINERS
BELOW: A hollowed-out log filled with shallow-rooting Cyclamen coum, *planted with a small-leaved ivy.*

An elegant show of snowdrops.

Penséer (*Viola* x *wittrockiana*)

Cyclamen (*Cyclamen persicum*)

Skimmia japonica 'Tansley Gem'

Dutch yellow crocus (*Crocus* x *luteus*)

Winter Plants

Due to the lack of competition, even a simple pot of cyclamen or snowdrops always looks surprisingly good in winter. For a more stylized effect you can plant bedding or bulbs around shrubs with interesting shapes or berries, provided that the lower branches have been pruned to make the flowers clearly visible. The limited winter palette does not mean that there is any lack in quality of blooms.

Specialty Pots

One of the great pleasures of container gardening is creating special themes. They include alpines, a world of scaled-down detail, the versatile herb garden, scented plants, and even mini-ponds. Container gardens can have plenty of gusto.

CUSTOMIZED CONTAINERS

Containers give you a wonderful opportunity to personalize your garden. French lavender grows in a stylish trough (left), while stripey pots add an individual touch (above).

Alpines

Alpines have special needs. They are high-altitude plants that, in their natural habitat, are covered in snow in winter. They are small and compact, and can withstand ferocious winds and rock falls. A bright position and excellent drainage are vital. A huge range of good alpine plants can be grown in special containers kept in the garden, where they will look very unusual. Covering the containers' gritty soil surface with a layer of pebbles and small rocks gives a feel of how they look in the wild, shows up their often delicate flowers, and makes a marvellous slug deterrent. You can combine them with some drought-tolerant plants, such as cacti and succulents, for a desert effect.

When buying plants it is worth visiting specialist alpine nurseries which will have a far bigger selection than garden centers, and possibly some of the latest finds. They will also give good tips for growing alpine plants.

HOUSELEEKS

TOP LEFT: *Get away from the idea that all plinths are naked without a classical statue. As this one shows, a bowl of houseleeks makes an extremely novel feature.*

THE TROUGH GARDEN

LEFT: *Alpines are addictive and you end up planting every bowl you can find. Note how the immediate area has been covered with gravel to imitate the scree of an alpine landscape.*

WALL PLANTINGS

RIGHT: *Some alpines love the rocky cracks on the tops of walls. Alternatively they can be safely placed here in shallow bowls. It raises them up to eye level. This collection includes* Sedum spathulifolium *'Purpureum',* Oxalis triangularis, *and* Campanula garganica *'Dickson's Gold'.*

Planting a shallow container

The key criteria for creating an alpine garden are plenty of drainage holes and free-draining compost. You can adapt an old sink or a stone trough, covering it with hypertufa. Alternatively coat it with adhesive and apply a mix of peat, builder's sand, and cement. Cover it with damp sacking, and then leave it to set. Carefully allocate its final position as the container can be extremely heavy to move when it has been planted.

1 *Put a layer of crocks in the bottom of the container. Then cover it with a mix of compost and coarse sand or fine gravel, at a 50:50 ratio. Add the plants.*

2 *Continue planting, carefully spreading out the roots. Add a generous layer of coarse sand or fine gravel around the crown of each plant for good drainage.*

3 *The final display with neatly displayed sempervivum, sedum, dianthus, and saxifrage.*

POTTED PROFUSION

LEFT: *The best place to stand pots is in a bright sunny position close to the kitchen. Regular pinching of most herbs, like this trio of basils, encourages them to fill out and become bushy.*

Golden marjoram
(*Origanum vulgare* 'Variegatum')

Rosemary (*Rosmarinus officinalis*)

Herbs in Containers

It is no great misfortune if you do not have space for a kitchen or vegetable garden. Herbs bring taste and freshness to any kitchen and can be grown in all kinds of containers. In fact, some herbs, such as mint, are best grown in pots to restrict their root run.

There is a huge range of herbs available. You can choose from around 18 varieties of basil (everything from the Italian kind to cinnamon basil, Thai basil, red-leaved basil, and spicy basil) to caraway and fenugreek. Just one or two pots can supply you with an easy-to-grow basic selection. Include French or Italian flat-leaved parsley (much stronger than the curly kind), chives, leafy cilantro coriander, marjoram or oregano, rosemary, and thyme. The annuals, such as basil, are easily grown from seed. Regular plantings over summer keep the kitchen well stocked.

Thyme (*Thymus*)

Oregano (*Origanum vulgare*)

A MEDICINAL COLLECTION

ABOVE: *For this attractive packed group of medicinal herbs you need rue, tansy, golden feverfew, and hyssop.*

Chives (*Allium schoenoprasum*)

Pot marigold (*Calendula officinalis*)

Golden variegated sage (*Salvia officinalis* 'Icterina')

WINDOWSILL FLAVORINGS

ABOVE: *Grow herbs in every available container. For the best show include some tall structural plants, such as rosemary (right).*

105

Scented Pots

Containers are a simple way of introducing scent to a garden – and with the right choice of plants you can have the smell of pineapples and marzipan. Pots can be moved around for maximum effect, and placed near doors or windows so that the smell can filter into the house. All it takes is a warm, sheltered spot, where the scent hangs on the air.

Scents are available all year round. The late winter strong scents start with the daphnes which, under glass in a garden room, really are stunning. The hardy evergreen *Daphne bholua* 'Jacqueline Postill' has pinkish or white flowers, and will only grow to about 6 ft (1.8 m) in a pot. Follow it with another hardy evergreen, *Daphne odora* 'Aureomarginata', with dark pink flowers, which grows to half the size. If you need another wave of perfume, grow the tender *Jasminum polyanthum*. If it grows too tall, prune it back after flowering, but give it fresh air over summer, standing it outside. Also provide plenty of tomato feed in summer to improve next year's show. The cooler the winter temperature once it is brought indoors in the fall, the later it will flower next spring.

SUMMER AND WINTER SCENTS
LEFT: *The excellent old varieties of heliotrope such as this 'Chatsworth' can be used as bedding plants in the summer, then potted up in the fall and brought indoors for winter. With a tomato feed they will keep on flowering.*

HYACINTHS
BELOW: *Plant hyacinths near seating areas where you can appreciate their amazingly rich scents.*

EVENING SCENTS
ABOVE: *Nicotiana plants have a wonderful evening scent. Include them in pots around a doorway or under a window.*

107

In summer you need plenty of lilies, and one of the old-fashioned heliotropes such as *Heliotropium* 'Princess Marina' for the wonderfully rich smell of marzipan. *Salvia rutilans* smells of fresh pineapples. For heady evening scents try nicotiana, and still one of the best annuals, night-scented stock. If you have a humid garden room, then pot up one of the tender hoyas. With a minimum winter temperature of 50°F (10°C) they will put out waxy, star-shaped flowers in showy clusters.

The season ends on a high. *Gladiolus callianthus* 'Murieliae' has white flowers with striking purple inner markings in fall, and a sweet scent. And for an inexpensive gift, plant up fall bowls of freesias. Easily raised, the buds open in winter or spring and their scent is quite exquisite.

SCENTED FOLIAGE

ABOVE: Scented-leafed pelargoniums should be placed where people gently brush past them, releasing their perfumes.

LAVENDER IN A POT

RIGHT: Lavenders, such as Lavandula angustifolia, *make fine plants for shape and scent.*

OVERPOWERING

LEFT: Lilium avratum *is one of the most easily grown, and most heavily-scented lilies. Indoors, it is overpowering, so place it outside under a window.*

THE SMELL OF CITRUS

RIGHT: You can grow everything from a kumquat to a lemon, especially with winter humidity.

Water Containers

If you want to add extra dimensions to your garden, you have to keep embellishing, and one of the best ingredients is water. You do not need huge swimming pools, ponds, or lakes – small containers dotted around the garden are simple and effective. There are a surprising number of ways to introduce water, even into small urban gardens, and containers make versatile and unusual features.

Wall fountains are easily installed, and traditionally involve a ready-made stone mask with water pouring out of the mouth into a ground-level basin, filled with large round pebbles, before being promptly recirculated. Modern versions may pour into a brightly colored watering can, nailed to a wall, then pour into another beneath, and one beneath that, in zigzagging descending layers, before being pumped back up to the start again. Alternatively, install a Japanese *shishi odoshi*, where water pours into and out of a hinged, hollow tube of cane, which makes a clacking sound as it rythmically strikes a stone.

Mini ponds are available as ready-made fiberglass units, but you can use wooden or plastic containers for the same effect. Create a circle of small ponds surrounding one large

WATER ECHOES

LEFT: *A circular pond is embellished by the addition of a small raised water container packed with large stones. The adjacent euphorbia, sedum, sage, and iris add lush green foliage.*

THE RUSTIC LOOK

RIGHT: *This barrel with an old-fashioned water pump makes an ideal ornamental feature for a small garden. The striped grasses highlight the scene.*

111

one in the center. For greater effect, cover the surounding ground with pebbles and stones. They can be permanently fixed in place by being set in concrete. To jazz up the area further, use brightly colored broken china and tiles. Note that unless the containers are about 18 in (45 cm) deep, adding fish is inadvisable because they will become trapped in ice when the temperature drops. You will almost certainly get plenty of frogs, though.

Plants for standing in ponds usually come ready-planted in small plastic baskets. Make sure that the soil surface is covered with stones to help weigh them down amd stop the soil from drifting away. Check that the plants added will grow to the right size for the area as some are furious spreaders – floating plants should cover only one-third of the water surface. Oxygenating plants, such as water starwort, Canadian waterweed, and water milfoil, will help to keep the water clean. Place the containers in bright sun, away from overhanging branches and the problem of falling leaves. Children should never be left unattended near water.

Yellow flag iris (*Iris pseudacorus*)

TUBS OF WATER

LEFT: *Ponds, whether large or small, are often best as magical sudden surprises, found half hidden behind tall wispy plants. These sunken tubs are surrounded by moisture-loving plants and ferns.*

GLAZED OVER

RIGHT: *Simple and highly effective: a glazed pot becomes a mini pond, complete with its own white water lily.*

THE OLD AND THE NEW

LEFT: *Bright, decorated pots can be used to enhance existing garden features. Here striped pots and plants frame an old wall mask. The yellow pots contain grape hyacinths, and the blue pot clipped box.*

BRIGHT AND CHEERFUL

RIGHT: *The best way to combat semi-shade is with plenty of bright colors. Silvery galvanized pots catch the light and highlight the cut flowers of orange gerberas and purple-blue larkspurs.*

Decorated Pots

Give your plain, terracotta pots a make-over. Choose colors that complement or contrast with the flowers for best effect. Do not be too subtle, as pale colors get lost; make the pots stand out with bold stripes in reds, purples, blues, and whites, or try painting them with with different size spots, hoops, or zigzags. Such decorations are an excellent way of highlighting small containers. When decorating large pots use simple patterns and solid colors to avoid over-complicating the effect.

To make a striped pot, begin by cleaning and drying it. Then apply an all-over background color, such as white. Next fix stripes of masking tape running up the side of the pot. Apply a second color, such as red, removing the tape when the paint has dried.

A TOUCH OF YELLOW

LEFT: *The startling yellow face of the sunflower is echoed by the yellow rim.*

You can add further colors, continuing in the same way. If you want to create a more home-made rustic look, paint by eye. The patterning does not have to be immaculate. Customizing your own pots in this way is much cheaper than looking for a pot with exactly the right color scheme, and certainly much more fun. Other suitable painting techniques include stencilling, sponging, and stippling.

Galvanized containers also make extremely good pots. They can be easily brightened up using controlled splashes of paint in whatever colors you wish. Golds and silvers look best.

Make a feature of your decorated containers, painting several pots and grouping them together boldly; individual decorated pots will look out of place on their own. Decorated pots can be used anywhere in the garden but look particularly attractive on windowsills and in doorways.

YELLOW AND BLUE POT

ABOVE: *Red pelargoniums are given a new lease of life in smartly colored pots.*

A VIBRANT DISPLAY

LEFT: *Brightly-colored parrot tulips need a sunny setting, such as these striking blue and white pots.*

WINTER COLOR

RIGHT: *White cyclamen, combined with vivid striped pots and young box plants, create an unusual display.*

SOUTH AMERICAN STYLE

LEFT: *Cacti and succulents come in all kinds of weird and wonderful shapes, from tiny pebblelike growths to elaborate candelabra. Ethnic-style pots add exactly the right finishing touch.*

SOFT HUES

ABOVE: *A perfect example of the range of simple patterns you can use to brighten up pots, from stripes and dots to regular wavy lines.*

119

The Garden
in Bloom

Border Basics

Beautiful borders must be orchestrated down to the last detail, from the tallest highlights to low-growing edging plants. In return, they will reward you with color and interest all through the year.

COLOR PALETTE

Lupins and roses set amongst purple sage and spurge (left) *make a lovely summer display, while red and yellow wallflowers* (above) *bring spring color to the garden.*

Border Style

A gorgeous border, filled with attractive plants, is an asset to any garden. Be sure to plan the border well before you start for the best results. A mixed border is the best option for most gardens, where planting has to look good all year round. Using small trees and shrubs as a framework, and finding space for bulbs and annuals as well as perennials, extends the life of a border well beyond the midsummer peak of a solely herbaceous version.

Traditionally, borders are created in front of a wall, hedge or fence, which forms a backdrop and dictates their rectangular shape. This arrangement imposes its own limitations on border design and in order for all the plants to be seen at their best, they have to be planted more or less in descending order of height.

Planting in this way still makes sense today, provided you don't stick to it too rigidly. Including a few taller plants with an open structure near to the front will break up any overly regimented effect – feathery meadow rue and astilbe are ideal.

SHADES OF SILVER AND WHITE

ABOVE: Airy **Crambe cordifolia,** *with clouds of tiny flowers, lends height to a vigorous silver and white border restrained by low box edging.*

SPRING MIXED BORDER

RIGHT: A walled garden in spring has borders filled with a tapestry of biennial wallflowers, pansies, tulips, and forget-me-nots, within a framework of flowering shrubs and trees, including Malus floribunda.

COTTAGE STYLE

ABOVE: These informal borders create a charming profusion of roses, lavatera, marguerites, and clematis leading to an archway swathed in sweet peas.

SINGING WITH COLOR

RIGHT: This traditional herbaceous border includes annual sunflowers that match Verbena bonariensis *for height and color contrast; they face sizzling dahlias 'Bishop of Llandaff' and 'Ellen Huston' with a shock of blue agapanthus lilies.*

FORMAL MEETS INFORMAL

ABOVE: This framework of variegated box and tall slim junipers is filled in with billowing shrub roses, sage, artemisia, rodgersia, and bergenia, and contained by a smooth grass path.

A ROSY PROSPECT

OPPOSITE: An exuberant rose border is underplanted with complementary colors – red valerian, pink erigeron, red fuchsias, and spires of purple campanula.

An island bed is simply a border that doesn't have a backdrop. Plant it up so that the tallest species are in the center, then it will look effective from whichever direction you see it.

Formal beds that are part of an overall pattern should also follow this rule – only the most informal cottage borders can cope with a seemingly random mix of heights and scale. It is worth taking the time and effort to plan out your beds and borders carefully. Once you have decided on an overall framework, you can select your plants and let your creativity run wild to create a border that is entirely your own.

Filling the Framework

Once the permanent framework of small trees and shrubs is in place, the fun starts. By filling the spaces in between with smaller shrubs and hardy perennials that flower in succession, the border will look good right through the seasons.

As the glorious blossom of spring-flowering shrubs, such as camellias, rhododendrons, daphnes, and broom begins to fade, the perennials take over. Lupins, peonies, and poppies are some of the biggest summer attractions, followed by delphiniums and phloxes. These in turn can be infilled with smaller species: lady's mantle, low-growing hardy geraniums, dianthus, and catmint.

For fall color, add Michaelmas daisies, dahlias, and Japanese anemones, backed up by flaming shrubs like *Photinia villosa* or sumac, if you have space.

Try to plan your border on paper first. Take into account each plant's effect on its neighbor and juxtapose different species for contrast – not just between flower color, but between foliage, texture, and form.

PERFECTLY PLANNED

OPPOSITE: *This well-made border has perennial plants arranged in descending order of height, starting with the tall plume poppy, followed by achillea and orange-red heleniums, and finishing with low clumps of sedums, catmint, geums, and hardy geraniums.*

COLOR CONTRAST

BELOW: *Yellow phlomis interwoven with vibrant purple French lavender makes a striking statement.*

Ground Cover

Where shrubs and trees predominate and cast a shade, ground-cover plants are invaluable. Not only are they happy in these conditions, but they are pretty to look at, too. The starry white flowers of sweet woodruff, and the creamy bells of *Symphytum grandiflorum* are well worth growing, but be wary of plants that can spread wildly, such as yellow archangel.

Most ground-cover species are fast growing and soon spread to cover bare earth and fill in gaps in the planting with a carpet of greenery. By forming a protective layer over the soil, they act as a living mulch and help the soil retain moisture and also deny weeds growing space. Ground-cover plants can also bring vital stability to a bare sloping site. They are low growing so can't be uprooted by strong winds and their spreading habit covers the soil and stops rain washing it away.

A PINK AND WHITE CARPET

BELOW: *Two varieties of deadnettle make a useful color contrast in a narrow border at the foot of a climbing rose. When the flowers have finished, there are still the variegated leaves to appreciate.*

Ground Cover

Where shrubs and trees predominate and cast a shade, ground-cover plants are invaluable. Not only are they happy in these conditions, but they are pretty to look at, too. The starry white flowers of sweet woodruff, and the creamy bells of *Symphytum grandiflorum* are well worth growing, but be wary of plants that can spread wildly, such as yellow archangel.

Most ground-cover species are fast growing and soon spread to cover bare earth and fill in gaps in the planting with a carpet of greenery. By forming a protective layer over the soil, they act as a living mulch and help the soil retain moisture and also deny weeds growing space. Ground-cover plants can also bring vital stability to a bare sloping site. They are low growing so can't be uprooted by strong winds and their spreading habit covers the soil and stops rain washing it away.

A PINK AND WHITE CARPET

BELOW: *Two varieties of deadnettle make a useful color contrast in a narrow border at the foot of a climbing rose. When the flowers have finished, there are still the variegated leaves to appreciate.*

SHADY COVER-UP

ABOVE: *Sweet woodruff is a charming shade-loving ground-cover plant that produces masses of starry white flowers in spring. The dried leaves smell of new-mown hay and were used in the past to scent laundry.*

WILD BORDER

LEFT: *Low-growing heartsease provides the ground-cover element in a wildflower planting of cornflowers, daisies, and field poppies.*

131

Honeysuckle (*Lonicera periclymenum*)

BERRY CASCADE

RIGHT: *The bright red berries of*
Lonicera periclymenum *'Serotina'*
make an attractive backdrop from late
summer and into fall. Here they
cascade into late-flowering rudbeckia
and petunias.

Backing Up

A wall or fence at the back of a border makes the perfect showcase for climbing plants and emphasizes the vertical aspects of your border. Climbing roses improve an old wall immensely, but remember that many of the old varieties flower just once. Pairing a rose with a clematis helps, as the latter tends to flower for longer, and the simpler flowers of the clematis are a foil for the more complexly structured roses. Add an old-fashioned honeysuckle for scent; if it's an evergreen one, so much the better for winter color.

Even if your border is bounded by a solid evergreen hedge, it's still possible to introduce splashes of color using creepers such as the flame flower or the annual canary creeper. Place the tallest plants close to the boundary – shrubs, trees, and tall perennials such as the plume poppy, globe thistles, and hollyhocks. If your border is deep, make a concealed path between boundary and plants so that you can get in to stake, prune, and deadhead as necessary.

ACCENTS OF YELLOW

ABOVE: Climbing yellow roses and honeysuckle have all but covered an old wall, and echo the yellow of the flag irises and shrub roses dotted amongst a sea of bronze fennel.

133

Clematis 'Pink Fantasy'

Vigorous *Clematis montana* scrambles through a laburnum tree to form a pretty canopy over a garden bench in spring.

Clematis Florida 'Sieboldii'

Clematis 'Madame Julia Correvon'

Clematis 'Fuji-musume'

Clematis

From the delicate nodding bells of *Clematis alpina* to the extravagant double flowers of some of the larger hybrids, the range of clematis is vast. They can be found flowering from spring to late fall, and after the last blooms are spent, there are still the fluffy seedheads to enjoy. The first starry flowers of *Clematis montana* appear in spring; *C. florida* 'Sieboldii' is another early cultivar, while 'Madame Julia Correvon' unfurls at the height of summer.

Close to the Edge

Having carefully planned your drifts of color and complementary plantings, you can introduce edging plants for a pretty finish. Soft billowy plants such as catmint, lady's mantle, little violas, dianthus, and corydalis will blur the precision of adjacent paths and conceal razor-sharp lawn edges.

The best edging plants are mat forming and evergreen, for a permanently defined boundary. If you want a neater result, clip them into shape from time to time. Try the pale mauve *Campanula poscharskyana* – deadheading it after the first flush of flowers in July often produces a second flowering later on. The Cape marigold has pretty daisylike flowers and dark-green leaves; *Anthemis punctata ssp. cupaniana* is similar, with filigreed gray leaves.

Where a border meets the lawn, lay a simple paved edge between the two, level with the lawn. This makes it easier to mow right up to the border's edge without trimming off any overhanging flowers and helps to keep the edging plants from spreading too far.

COLOR RIGHT UP TO THE EDGE

ABOVE: Nepeta *'Six Hills Giant' forms a margin of dense color when planted with red valerian.*

FOAMING FLOWERS

RIGHT: Lady's mantle marks the edge of a border with a froth of greeny-yellow flowers. Its attractive leaves are slightly cup-shaped and often hold a silvery dewdrop in early morning.

PURPLE HAZE

OPPOSITE: A mass of catmint forms a colorful border to a rose bed. Clip back hard if it starts to get out of hand.

Balancing the Border

In planning a border, you must consider how each plant can contribute to the overall effect. Think carefully about how plants will fit into your scheme. Concentrate on creating contrasts in shape and form, in color or texture – spiky purple liatris next to a cloud of hazy white gypsophila; yellow achillea tempered by the plumy flowers of *Artemisia lactiflora*. Nursery catalogs and reference books are invaluable: it's no use deciding to contrast a pink phlox with a blue hardy geranium if they are not in flower at the same time.

Except where a large plant is intended as a highlight or focus within the border, planting a single specimen is rarely successful. As in flower arranging, the golden rule is to group plants in odd numbers: three, five, or seven at the most.

In a long border, repeating groupings of plants will give your design a rhythm in the vast medley of colors, textures, and shapes.

Peony
(*Paeonia*)

A LITTLE REPETITION

ABOVE: Repeat plantings of tall clary sage confer a degree of formality and cohesion to this border.

A WELL-BALANCED THEME

LEFT: Spires of lupins and delphiniums contrast with the loose white pompons of a climbing rose, while artemisia and sage link the planting at a lower level.

Border Highlights

Interrupting a planting with a highlight or specimen plant is a clever gardener's strategy to focus the attention. Imagine an architectural plant such as a yucca, with its wrinkled trunk, spiky foliage, and panicles of bell-shaped flowers, rising from a bed of unassuming and delicate hardy geraniums and drifts of catmint. Similarly spiky specimens include phormiums and red-hot pokers, which can introduce an element of surprise into the most well-modulated border and bring a tropical feel with their exotic appearance.

Vast candelabra of *Eryngium pandanifolium* which spread to 8 ft (2.4 m) across or clouds of *Crambe cordifolia* can be used to punctuate a border like a series of exclamation marks. Grasses make ideal highlight plants in a flower border, their sharply defined leaves providing a graphic contrast to soft flower shapes. In a big bed, pampas grass can look magnificent. Surrounding it with other plants will hide away any untidy lower leaves.

For a small border try miscanthus. *M. sinensis* has purply silver flowers while 'Zebrinus' has golden cross-banding on its leaves. Grasses also add movement to a border as they ripple in the breeze.

LOOK AT ME!
RIGHT: Red-hot pokers make a bold border statement. The yellow and white species would be more suitable for a restrained color scheme.

MAKING A STATEMENT
OPPOSITE: Two-tone Phormium *'Sundowner' stands out from a sea of green composed of sedum,* Nicotiana *'Lime Green' and clumps of low-growing grasses.*

Shapely Shrubs

The framework of a mixed border is formed by small trees and shrubs. As well as creating permanent structure, they can also contribute a great deal of color and a wealth of interesting shapes.

AN ASSORTMENT OF SHRUBS
Clever planting makes use of flowering shrubs such as the colorful blue ceanothus (left) *and the sun-loving* Potentilla fruticosa *'Primrose Beauty'* (above).

Small Trees and Shrubs

A tree is possibly a garden's greatest asset. As well as being visually dramatic, a mature tree will attract a variety of wildlife into your garden.

Trees and shrubs need to be in place before you start to fill the border with smaller plants. Your first consideration should be height. A tree that is too tall disrupts the garden's balance and may block the light. To help you choose, reference books and nursery catalogs indicate a tree's height at maturity and also after five years, which will give you a good idea of how quickly it grows.

Shape and spread are important factors, too. Some trees, such as *Cupressus sempervirens* 'Swane's Gold', which grows to 13 ft (3.9 m) are nearly columnar; others, such as *Carpinus betulu*s 'Fastigiata' – 10 ft (3 m) after 20 years – are conical. The Indian bean tree is nearly as wide as it is tall, as is *Styrax japonicus*.

Once you have considered these factors and narrowed the choice, flowers, fruit, bark, and fall leaf color can all influence your decision about which tree or shrub to incorporate into your border design.

LIT FROM BEHIND

RIGHT: Low fall sunshine suffuses the leaves of Corylus maxima *'Purpurea' with an extra burst of color and throws the veining into sharp relief.*

144

A PATCHWORK OF COLORS

LEFT: *Large trees such as oak and blue cedar, filled in with shrubs including spiraea and berberis, illustrate the enormous variation in color, shape, and size of trees and shrubs.*

MAGNIFICENT MAGNOLIAS

BELOW: *Magnolias bear their candle-flame flowers early in the year. The blooms are vulnerable to frost, but it is a risk well worth taking for this glorious display.*

Evergreens

For year-round color and structure, evergreens are hard to beat. Typically dark green specimens such as yew, holly, and Western red cedar look wonderful with yellow-green species such as *Cryptomeria japonica* 'Elegans Aurea' or blue-green spruce, or underplanted with lower-growing variegated shrubs such as euonymus.

Evergreens look their best mixed with other plants. Combining them with deciduous species makes an open, varied framework that has the advantage of some winter color. Try to use evergreens with additional attributes. Some have attractive flowers. The strawberry tree has clusters of scented white flowers in fall, that often sit side-by-side with its fruits.

Conifers are always interesting. Try *Abies koreana*, which is a slow-growing pyramid-shaped tree with dark shiny needles that have a silver underside and lovely purple-blue cones held upright like candles on a Christmas tree.

Euonymus fortunei 'Emerald 'n' Gold'

147

Shrubs for Small Beds

Shrubs form a wonderful framework for a border but a small bed can become swamped by vigorous shrubs. Fortunately there are plenty of shrubs that are naturally compact or slow growing; others can be kept in check – and often enhanced – by pruning.

Keep box small by frequent clipping; it is an ideal candidate for informal topiary. Shape it into mounds or crisp border edgings. Hebes are useful evergreens: many are low-growing, even ground-cover plants and fit perfectly into a small mixed border. *Hebe* 'Autumn Glory' flowers continuously throughout summer into fall; cutting it back in spring every four years keeps it in trim.

Don't forget that lavender is a small shrub that can be clipped into loose mounds which then become fuzzy with flowers over the summer. As it has a tendency to become woody, take cuttings every winter to replace offending plants. Leave rosemary to grow into an informal hedge or choose a prostrate form such as 'Jackman's Prostrate'.

THE KINDEST CUT
ABOVE: Both lavender and the silver-leaved curry plant benefit from an annual clipping – lavender in mid-spring (then again lightly in fall, if necessary); cut back frost damage to curry plant in spring.

THE STARS OF THE SMALL BORDER
RIGHT: Hebes are obliging little shrubs, with neat evergreen foliage and flowers that last all summer long and on into fall. Hebe x franciscana 'Variegata' is a bushy cultivar that is half hardy.

Variegated and Silver Plants

Silver and gray are hard-working colors in the border. They can extend a limited palette or temper extremes of color to make them easier on the eye. Gray foliage also complements a muted scheme. Shrubs with silver or gray leaves – lavender, santolina, artemisia, and phlomis – are also suitable for dry, sunny sites as they are less vulnerable to scorching.

Variegated shrubs are more delicate, and some species lose their contrasting foliage if planted in too sunny a spot. Use them to animate a bed of unrelieved green or to lift a gloomy corner – variegated hollies are ideal for this purpose. *Ilex aquifolium* 'Silver Queen' has striking white-edged leaves that are true to form whatever the conditions.

Euonymus are tough little shrubs and some of the variegated forms have the added bonus of a seasonal color change: the golden edges of the leaves of *E. fortunei* 'Emerald 'n' Gold' flush pink in winter.

Lychnis coronaria

DUAL ACTION

ABOVE: **Cornus alba** *'Sibirica Variegata' has green and creamy-white leaves, shed to reveal scarlet winter stems, ensuring its place on two counts.*

Convolvulus cneorum

Pinks
(*Dianthus* cv.)

Perpetual stocks
(*Matthiola incana* cv.)

Lavender
(*Lavandula* cv.)

Curry plant
(*Helichrysum italicum*)

Catmint
(*Nepeta* x *faassenii*)

PURPLE, GOLD, AND SILVER

RIGHT: *Stems of a variegated weigela are interwoven with golden dogwood and a purply bronze backdrop of berberis in this colorful collection.*

Cotton lavender (*Santolina chamae-cyparissus*)

Senecio 'Sunshine'

Ivy (*Hedera colchica* 'Dentata Variegata')

Cotoneaster atropurpureus 'Variegatus'

Hosta fortunei var. 'Aureomarginata'

Pineapple mint (*Mentha suaveolens* 'Variegata')

Variegated ground elder (*Aegopodium podagraria* 'Variegatum')

Shrub Roses

No mixed border would be complete without roses for color, scent, and beautiful flowers. With few exceptions, modern shrub roses will bloom from early summer to fall (diligent deadheading will encourage them toward the end of the season), thus earning their place in the border more readily than an old rose that looks glorious for just two weeks a year.

If you yearn for the old-fashioned charm of near-globular blooms packed with petals, or curiously quartered flowers, rose breeders today have managed to combine these qualities with a repeat-flowering habit. Varieties such as 'Graham Thomas', 'Leander', and 'Charles Rennie Mackintosh' keep the style of old roses but flower more than once.

Roses look their best in a mixed planting but can be segregated to create a formal rose bed. In the border their bare lower stems can be concealed by companion plants, such as lavender, catmint, and hardy geraniums.

ROSES UNRESTRAINED

LEFT: *Pink 'Mary Rose' and yellow 'Graham Thomas' are complemented by purple pansies and two weeping forms of trees – maple and pear.*

AN ANCIENT ROSE

BELOW: *The striped flowers of* Rosa gallica *'Versicolor' – one of the oldest roses in cultivation – are borne for a few weeks in summer.*

OLD MEETS NEW

ABOVE RIGHT: Rosa *'Graham Thomas' has large old-fashioned double flowers in a warm shade of yellow that are produced more or less continuously.*

A BED OF ROSES

ABOVE: *Here roses have been used in a formal setting, crisply edged with box and underplanted with antirrhinums.*

Flowering Shrubs

There is a wealth of flowering shrubs that will bring almost trouble-free color and form to a border. One of the most undemanding shrubs renowned for its flowers is the hydrangea. Hydrangeas have a long flowering season – from early summer to fall – rarely need pruning, and flourish in dappled shade. Depending on variety, flowers can be nearly spherical (mopheads), arranged in flat plates with the largest florets at the edge (lacecaps), or produced in long panicles. Frost is their worst enemy, but although it can decimate the flower buds, it rarely kills the plant.

The evergreen *Viburnum tinus* produces flowers from mid-fall through the winter. As they age they become stained with pink, and are followed by dusty blue berries. Another evergreen, *Daphne acutiloba,* has white flowers in summer and scarlet berries in fall – it is ideal for small spaces as it grows very slowly, reaching 5 ft (1.5 m) after many years. For a sweetly scented version, choose D. *mezereum*, which is deciduous.

Laurustinus
(*Viburnum tinus*)

DELICATE DROPS

FAR LEFT: Fuchsia magellanica *is one of the hardiest fuchsias and flowers for months. In mild areas it can reach 10 ft (3 m) high.*

BERRIED TREASURE

CENTER LEFT: Skimmia japonica *has sprays of small white flowers in spring that are followed by scarlet berries on the female plant if there is a male plant nearby.*

SHELTERED SHRUBS

LEFT: A high wall provides the perfect habitat for a tall blue-flowered ceanothus in a mixed shrubbery. Pink-flowered varieties also exist.

FULL-BLOWN BEAUTY

*BELOW: The vibrant pink mophead
flowers of* Hydrangea macrophylla
*'Altona' gradually turn crimson or even
purple as the fall advances. The shrub
grows to about 3 ft (90 cm).*

Like hydrangeas, fuchsias deserve to be more widely planted. Hardy varieties
are strong enough to form a hedge; the dwarf species make good edging plants.
The variegated form of *Fuchsia magellanica* constantly changes color, vacillating
between gray-green and bright pink and intensifying in spring and again in fall.

Californian lilacs appreciate a south-facing wall: *Ceanothus* x *veitchianus* has
clusters of deep blue flowers in late spring and makes a lovely show.

COLOR IN FALL

LEFT: *For a spectacular fall shrubbery, include specimens such as dogwoods whose bright red stems are revealed as their leaves fall, and heavily berried cotoneaster – here in a weeping form.*

Planting a shrub

Container-grown shrubs can be planted at any time of year, provided the ground is not frozen solid or completely dried out. If possible, dig over a large area of the border first, otherwise water may drain into the less densely packed soil in the hole and rot the shrub's roots. Water the shrub thoroughly before you remove it from the pot. When you put it in the ground, make sure that the soil comes up to exactly the same level on the stem as it did in the pot. If the area is dry, water regularly until the shrub is properly established.

1 *Dig a hole slightly larger than the container and break up the bottom of the hole with a fork. Add a sprinkling of bonemeal and water the ground if dry.*

2 *Let the water drain away, then plant the shrub. Gently fill in the soil around the rootball, then firm it down with your feet. Water well.*

157

Blue and pink hydrangeas can be persuaded to change
color according to the acidity or alkalinity of the soil.

Rhododendron yakushimanum

French lavender (*Lavandula stoechas*)

Heliotropium arborescens 'Marine'

Magnolia grandiflora 'Exmouth'

Flowering Shrubs

Flowering shrubs come in a vast array of shapes and sizes, from the tender cherry pie plant more often used as summer bedding, to magnificent spring-flowering magnolias, and taking in many others along the way – including lavenders, rhododendrons, and hydrangeas. They are also some of the most trouble-free garden plants, provided that you match their requirements from the start.

Essential Perennials

A garden needs perennials to add structure, color, and interest year after year. Use them as the basis for your planting scheme and watch them flower to give you pleasure through the seasons.

CLOUDS OF COLOR
Reliable perennials are the mainstay of the border, such as Lychnis coronaria *'Alba'* (left) *and* Dianthus *'Icomb'* (above).

ESSENTIAL PERENNIALS

TWO TONES OF PURPLE
RIGHT: The intense rich purple of Salvia nemorosa *is softened by a background haze of lilac cranesbill flowers.*

POINTING THE WAY
BELOW: These traditional herbaceous borders frame a grassy path leading to a stretch of water.

Herbaceous Perennials

Plants that die back each winter and lie dormant until spring are known as herbaceous perennials. Unlike shrubs, they do not make woody growth; instead, their soft stems are cut back by frost and snow. Traditional herbaceous borders were largely a summer phenomenon; today it seems more sensible to combine herbaceous perennials with shrubs, trees, bulbs, and annuals for a longer-lasting, more balanced planting.

To many gardeners herbaceous perennials are synonymous with flowers: delphiniums, poppies, lupins, salvias, penstemons, and asters, to name but a few. If you grow these you will never be short of cut blooms for the house. Some of the larger species, such as delphiniums, hollyhocks, anchusas, and verbascums, may need staking to keep flower spikes upright; others will gradually decline in flowering power unless they are lifted and divided every few years. A few species need the protection of a dry mulch or a layer of straw during cold weather – but other than that, they are a pretty undemanding group.

SHAPE AND COLOR
ABOVE: In this border, leaf shape is just as important as flower color. Spiky iris and shiny rounded bergenia leaves underline a pink and red theme of lavatera, salvia, dahlias seen with the small red flowers of Knautia macedonica.

163

Spring Perennials

One of the first perennials to greet the spring is lungwort, with its welcome sprays of blue and pink bells and bristly silver-spotted leaves. There are white, blue, and red varieties and they make good ground cover for shady corners.

Following closely on from the lungworts come two species with flowers arranged on delicately arching stems: Solomon's seal and dicentra. In a sheltered spot dicentras will bloom for weeks. At about the same time, leopard's bane sends out dandelion-like flowers for a cheerful splash of gold.

At ground level there are early primroses, sprays of blue brunnera held above perfect heart-shaped leaves, and the creamy bells of *Symphytum grandiflorum*. This low-growing member of the comfrey family is a useful ground-cover plant in shade and produces flowers even in the depths of winter.

Spurges are more unconventional spring- and summer-flowering perennials. The flower heads of *Euphorbia characias* ssp. *wulfenii* appear in late spring and are an arresting sight on the mature plants, which can reach 6 ft (1.8 m).

SPRING IS ON THE WAY

ABOVE: Early-flowering lungwort produces pink and blue flowers on the same stem.

SPRING SPURGES

RIGHT: The curious greeny yellow bottle-brush flowers of Euphorbia characias *ssp.* wulfenii *are interwoven here with stems of red valerian.*

PURE AT HEART

RIGHT: Dicentra spectabilis *'Alba'*, the white form of bleeding heart, has hanging flowers carefully spaced in a delicate arch.

LEADING INTO SUMMER

BELOW: Late-flowering spring tulips and the horned pansy linger on as early summer perennial cornflowers come into bloom.

Summer Perennials

Summer borders should be crammed with your favorite plants: double peonies packed with petals and elegant single varieties that date back to ancient China; obliging aquilegias that will put up with sun or shade; and the handsome monkshood, alongside clumps of pastel phlox.

Delphiniums are one of the classic summer border plants and come in shades from midnight blue to dusky pink and creamy white. They can grow as tall as 7 ft (2.1 m) and require staking against high winds and heavy rains. Delphiniums rely on helpful neighbors to disguise any untidiness as their flowering peak passes: phlox in matching tones of pink and white, subtle pincushion flowers of astrantia, and the less vibrant varieties of achillea.

From late spring, poppies put on an extravagant display. Perennial oriental poppies have flowers as big as dinner plates, with petals as stiff as a ballerina's skirts, in pink, orange, white, and red. They need staking as discreetly as

Golden rod (*Solidago* sp.)

SHIFTING SEASONS

RIGHT: The appearance of the elegant spurred flowers of aquilegia marks the transition from spring to summer.

SUMMER DAISIES

OPPOSITE: Yellow heleniums, yellow and white shasta daisies, and the shaggy cultivar 'Esther Read', mingle with golden rod and a striking loosestrife.

IN FULL BLOOM

BELOW: Delphiniums and foxgloves compete for height with opium poppies and white-flowered lychnis in a flower-filled summer border.

possible and should be cut back after flowering to tidy up the border, though there is an argument for leaving some of the attractive seedheads still standing.

Salvias are ideal for brightening up borders in late summer. Intensely blue *Salvia patens* grows to about 2 ft (60 cm). At the opposite end of the scale is *S. involucrata* 'Bethellii' which can reach 5 ft (1.5 m) and has shocking pink and purple flowers. Physostegia is another late-flowering perennial with neat spires of pink or white flowers.

LEFT: *Lupins are members of the pea family and have typical sweet-pea-shaped flowers in shades of orange, yellow, red, and blue, plus attractive palmlike leaves.*

Staking perennials

There's no escaping the fact that many of the taller perennials need a little bit of assistance to stand up to strong winds or heavy rain. Canes and garden twine are the time-honored, and inexpensive, tools for tieing up plants. They need not look unsightly, rearranging the foliage after they are firmly in place helps to camouflage them.

1 *Space four canes or stakes evenly around the edge of the plant, pushing them in to a depth of 4–6 in (10–15 cm).*

2 *Encircle canes and plant with string, looping it around each cane to secure it. Make the first circle near the ground and a second higher up.*

These gorgeous oriental poppies show off their colors in a summer garden.

Papaver orientale 'Perry's White'

Papaver orientale 'Curlilocks'

Welsh poppy (*Meconopsis cambrica*)

Papaver orientale 'Cedric Morris'

GARDENER'S CHOICE

Poppies

For a few wonderful weeks each summer, perennial oriental poppies are queens of the borders, with their crêpe-paper petals, sooty black stamens, and furry green buds. There are around 60 cultivars available. 'Curlilocks' has deeply fringed petals, while 'Perry's White' is, in fact, faintly suffused with pink. The Welsh poppy thrives in shady borders and flowers from spring until the first frosts. *Meconopsis betonicifolia* is a gorgeous blue.

171

SIMPLE BEAUTY

LEFT: *Japanese anemones form impressive clumps if left undisturbed and put on a welcome display of simple five- or six-petalled flowers in fall.*

A LAST BURST OF COLOR

RIGHT: *Rusty orange heleniums revive a border in fall, and tall plume poppies are still going strong. The pink crinum lilies are fall-flowering bulbs.*

PINK AND RED ASTERS

BELOW LEFT: *The New England aster is a native North American plant that flowers in fall.*

Fall Perennials

Certain plants signal the turn of the year like no others. The delicately simple flowers of the Japanese anemone are an indication that the days are turning cooler and the rich plums and pinks of Michaelmas daisies are a colorful reminder that fall is here.

In fact there is a preponderance of daisies at this time of year, all native to North America – some to the plains, others to woodland margins and damp meadows. The drop in temperature prompts heleniums to bring a late burst of color to the garden, with their prominent cone-shaped centers and turned-back petals in shades of rust, bronze, and orange. Echinaceas share the same flower shape but extend the color range with whites and purples. Rudbeckias are a cheerful yellow with black centers. Even the tiny fluffy clusters of eupatorium are part of the great daisy family.

Fleshy-leaved sedums produce flat pink and purple flowerheads in fall, and upright species such as red-hot pokers and liatris are still making a good show when the days are cooler.

GLAMOROUS GRASSES
LEFT: *Tall variegated miscanthus and lower-growing mounds of festuca form an informal planting with soft gray and yellow candelabras of mullein. Grasses are important components of fall and winter gardens.*

175

Annuals
and Bulbs

Annuals are the perfect solution for filling gaps in borders or boosting a more permanent color scheme, while bulbs usefully extend the flowering season and add stunning summer highlights.

ANNUALS IN PINK AND WHITE

Pink and white flowers of annual cosmos (left and above) are complemented by its ferny foliage, and are combined here with similarly shaped Japanese anemones.

Spring Bulbs

Spring bulbs play an important role in extending the seasonal interest in a mixed border, flowering when most herbaceous perennials are safely tucked away underground. Then they themselves modestly die back and disappear for a whole year, leaving the stage free for the next display.

Because of their fleshy structure, most bulbs need to be planted in well-drained soil. If you are at all doubtful, it is always worth putting a layer of sand or grit at the bottom of the planting hole before you add the bulb.

After the plants have flowered, go around the garden and deadhead spent flowers immediately to stop the plants diverting precious resources from bulb to seed production, but let the foliage die back naturally before cutting it back close to the ground. Resist the temptation to tidy up: tieing leaves into neat bunches restricts the supply of food to the bulb and so affects next year's performance. Where bulbs are growing in a lawn, try to refrain from mowing until six weeks after flowering.

A TYPICAL SPRING BORDER
LEFT: Perfumed hyacinths form a scented island amid a sea of grape hyacinths, aubrieta, and dwarf tulips.

BLUE AND WHITE STARS
BELOW LEFT: The charming flowers of Chionodoxa forbesii *are perfect for the front of a border.*

BELLS OF AZURE BLUE
BELOW RIGHT: Scilla siberica *is an early-flowering bulb that likes dappled shade.*

Daffodil
(*Narcissus* cv.)
and grape hyacinth
(*Muscari* sp.)

Many jonquil types of narcissus are sweetly scented. Other scented flowers include bluebells, some snowdrops – which are faintly honey-scented – the crocuslike sternbergia and some crocuses themselves.

Daffodils and snowdrops increase in numbers if left to their own resources and will need dividing every few years to improve flowering. Tulips do better if lifted after the leaves have died and stored in a dry place until fall, when they can be planted again, ready for a spring display.

BANDS OF COLOR

ABOVE: Tall daffodils, pink daisies, and red tulips create distinct levels of color. Taller unopened tulip buds prevent the effect from looking too contrived.

A CLOUD OF GOLD

RIGHT: A generous drift of Narcissus 'Peeping Tom'. For a natural effect, be generous with your planting – a single row of flowers looks unnatural.

Summer Bulbs

Summer-flowering bulbs, corms, and tubers provide interesting highlights in a border. Some, such as the Himalayan lily *Cardiocrinum giganteum* or forms of gladioli, are quite large, producing spectacular architectural plants. Lilies look elegantly formal in a restrained planting and equally at home in a more relaxed scheme – especially with shrub roses and phlox.

For strong color accents look no further than the fiery crocosmia. They soon form bold clumps that benefit from dividing every few years. Dahlias, too, are hardly shy and reserved, and come in some of the brightest reds and searing pinks around. You can have a lot of fun choosing their flower shapes, from spherical to spiky cactus shapes to pompons and water lily styles.

The striking globes of allium flower heads in metallic pinks and purples look dramatic grown through perennials in full bloom. Don't rush to deadhead them either, as the seedheads are spectacular silvered with frost on a winter morning.

ORANGE CRUSH

LEFT: *Yellow achillea and rudbeckia pick up the flush of yellow on* Crocosmia x crocosmiiflora.

COLORS COLLIDE

BELOW: *Orange and red crocosmias in a late-summer garden are daringly paired with a sugar-pink lavatera and yellow ligularia.*

Virginal white trumpets of *Lilium longiflorum* tower above low-growing white roses and white bearded iris.

Lilium nepalense

Lilium 'Marie North'

Lilium 'Peggy North'

Lilium pardalinum

Lilies

Lilies are among the most beautiful garden flowers and many are unsurpassingly fragrant. Some have trumpet-shaped flowers, others are star-shaped, while the petals of turk's cap lilies are attractively reflexed. Most lilies prefer open sun to flower but with a little shade at their roots, helpfully supplied by adjacent plants in a mixed border. For maximum impact, grow them in clumps but divide them every three to four years.

Summer Annuals

Annual plants germinate, produce flowers, set seed, and die, all within the space of a year. This rapid lifecycle makes them ideal for bringing almost instant color effects into the garden, and for filling in space until perennials grow to maturity, or for covering up gaps where a plant has failed.

There is a profusion of shapes, sizes, and colors available, with species to suit all sites and soils – and they are all easily raised from seed, making annuals one of the cheapest options. Many species will self-seed, saving you the trouble after the initial sowing. This often brings about a successful juxtaposition of flowers and colors as they spring up at random during the flowering year.

When the soil has warmed up sufficiently in spring, annual seed can be sown directly in the ground where the plants are to flower. Dig the soil over a week or two beforehand, then rake off any stones and weeds, and make short furrows to sow the seed in. Even if you are planting in fluid shapes and drifts, sow in straight rows within the area so that seedlings and weeds are easily identified.

Sweet William (*Dianthus barbatus*)

IN THE PINK

LEFT: *Annual nicotiana in pink-and-white and deep cerise are complemented by an underplanting of purple petunias in a pretty summer border.*

PERFECTLY PINK

LEFT: *This pink petunia has been partnered with gray-leaved helichrysum for a subtle contrast. Raise petunias from seed or buy them as bedding plants to put out when frosts are finished.*

Planting out bedding plants

Bedding plants are readily available in garden centers or even by mail order. When choosing trays of plants, avoid any that are in full flower, as they are already at their peak and so are unlikely to last too well once they are planted in the garden.

Always harden bedding plants off in a cold frame, for seven to ten days, before planting them outside, and make sure that all danger of frost is past in your area.

1 *Potting compost has a tendency to dry out, so soak bedding plants in a tray of water for around 20 minutes before planting.*

2 *Arrange pot-grown plants in their final positions, then dig each hole, remove the pot and firm in the plant. Divide up strip-grown plants before planting.*

SUN-LOVING CALIFORNIANS

ABOVE: California poppies are easy to grow. Sow them in full sun where they will thrive.

Annuals such as clarkia, marigolds, California poppies, cornflowers, and nigella can all be sown in fall if you really want to get ahead for the following year.

If you leave it too late to sow, or simply haven't got time, then plenty of annuals are sold as bedding plants: sweet-scented petunias, tall Canterbury bells, and frilly China asters, to name but a few.

KITCHEN GARDEN MARIGOLDS

ABOVE: Pot margiolds add striking annual color to this kitchen garden.

SELF PROMOTION

LEFT: Annual poppies are notoriously efficient at self-seeding. They make a welcome contribution to many gardens.

189

Fall Annuals

Later-flowering species tend to put on a brighter show, drawing attention to themselves in an explosion of color before the colder months. Flowers are scarlet, sizzling orange, and searing yellow. Think of daisylike annual coreopsis and gaillardia, and brassy African marigolds, which are all in full flower well into fall.

Nothing could offer a greater contrast in shape and form than love-lies-bleeding. It produces blood-red tassels and will carry on doing so until the first frosts hit. There is also a lime-green variety for a cooler effect.

Nasturtiums flower bravely until felled by frost. Some varieties are bushy, others trailing; all flower best on poor soil, so don't be tricked into giving them a nutritious mulch.

Annual seedheads contribute to the borders at this time of year: horned cases of nigella; paper-thin moons of honesty after the seeds have fallen; and smooth gray-green poppy seedheads like pepper pots, which may even rattle in the breeze until all the seed is cast.

LATE BORDER COLOR
LEFT: Nasturtiums and zinnias contribute hot pinks and orange to a border color scheme until the first frosts.

BETWEEN THE SEASONS
RIGHT: This white border is on the cusp of late summer and fall, with tall, fragrant annual Nicotiana sylvestris, *cosmos, and marguerites. Clumps of variegated hosta leaves pick up the color of the marguerites.*

Pot marigold (*Calendula officinalis*)

Nemesia strumosa 'Carnival series'

Mallow (*Lavatera*)

Annuals bring a glorious riot of color to a summer border.

Love-in-a-mist (*Nigella damascena*)

Annuals

Annuals are inherently useful in the garden. They are fast growing and add almost instant color. You can use them like a painter's palette to create drifts and gradations of color in the garden wherever it's needed. You will also have masses of flowers for cutting and – another bonus – many species are scented, such as petunias, stocks, and nicotiana.

Color Palettes

Designing a border with a particular color theme can be fun and quite a challenge. Choose your favorite colors and decorate your garden in the same way as you would your home.

OPPOSITES ATTRACT

A red and pink garden (left) is not for the faint hearted! Hot colors, such as shocking pink (above), bring cheer to any garden.

SOME LIKE IT HOT

RIGHT: Orange alstroemeria and red rudbeckia blaze away in a border with creamy day lilies and tall yellow verbascum. Add some gray or silver foliage if you want a less shocking effect.

Daffodil (*Narcissus* 'Tête-à-Tête')

Daffodil (*Narcissus* 'February Gold')

Sweet pea (*Lathyrus odoratus*)

Rose (*Rosa* 'Etoile de Hollande')

Wattle (*Acacia* sp.)

Geranium (*Pelargonium* 'Cascade')

Hot Borders

Under a blazing summer sun, a border composed of yellow, orange, and red flowers burns fiercely; but once the sun starts to drop, then those very same colors will glow with a luminous brightness that intensifies as dusk falls. Such hot colors, by their nature, catch the eye first in any planting. They appear closer than they really are, so must be used carefully where space is limited.

A border that echoes the colors of the setting sun might comprise a base of yellow pansies, with tiers of yellow day lilies and flat-headed achillea, studded with orange and scarlet. Fiery red dahlias, orange nasturtiums, heleniums, and antirrhinums will invigorate and intensify the underlying yellow.

For an early spring border, orange and red wallflowers, daffodils, and scarlet tulips will create a similar, although less forceful, effect in the weaker spring sunlight.

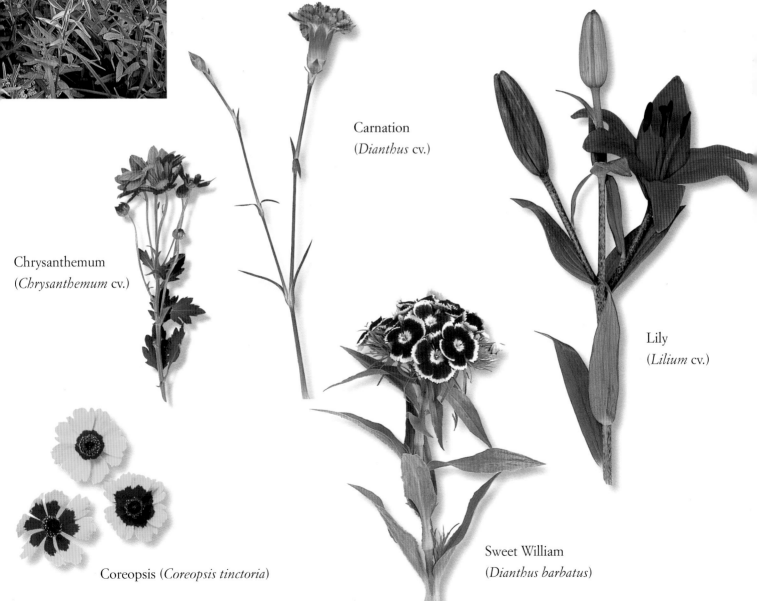

Carnation
(*Dianthus* cv.)

Chrysanthemum
(*Chrysanthemum* cv.)

Lily
(*Lilium* cv.)

Coreopsis (*Coreopsis tinctoria*)

Sweet William
(*Dianthus barbatus*)

197

YELLOW UNRESTRAINED

RIGHT: This cottage-style border is packed with shades of yellow from annual African and French marigolds, in front of a cool green ivy-clad pavilion.

HOT AND COLD PLANTING

OPPOSITE: Variegated cornus and icy white Japanese anemones are the backdrop for a hot yellow fringe of blanket flowers and late-summer daisies.

Yellow Borders

Yellow is the color of sunshine and cheerfulness. It has an instant impact wherever it is placed, bringing light and brilliance to the garden.

The yellows of spring daffodils, winter aconites, winter jasmine, pale primroses, and cowslips are cool tones, with a hint of green. They are a heartening sight after a long drab winter and promise better things to come.

Spring yellows are easy to use without considering too closely their effect on companion plants, unlike the bolder tones of summer-flowering species. Achillea, crocosmia, lysimachia, sunflowers, golden rod, and African marigolds, all look splendid mixed with oranges and reds on scorching summer days. As summer turns slowly into fall, a yellow border appears gentler as the daylight weakens and the flowers become a welcome reminder of the sun.

Chrysanthemum
(*Chrysanthemum* cv.)

Summer daisies are complemented by the silver foliage of the adjacent plants.

Sneezeweed (*Helenium* 'Wyndley')

Tulipa tarda

Yarrow (*Achillea filipendulina* 'Gold Plate')

Sunflower (*Helianthus* cv.)

Yellow Flowers

From the earliest crocuses and daffodils, to late-summer daisies such as rudbeckias, yellow flowers are well represented in the garden. Choose from a varied palette that encompasses the pure sunshine yellow of the annual sunflower, the brassy gold of achillea, and cream-tipped dwarf yellow tulips, to take you through the seasons.

Red Borders

Red is gorgeous, dramatic, and passionate but definitely not for the faint-hearted. It is a hot color and will 'advance' a planting, so plan its use with care.

It may not be easy to keep a red theme going all through the seasons, but you can plan a series of predominantly red highlights that will bring your garden alive. A border of scarlet poppies, *Crocosmia* 'Lucifer', red geum, roses, and red-hot pokers will peak in midsummer, and could be superceded by a wave of red nasturtiums, crimson fuchsias, and the scarlet dahlia 'Bishop of Llandaff'. The latter has deep purplish bronze leaves, which suit a red border better than typical summery green foliage. Build up the bronze foliage with feathery bronze fennel, purple-leaved heuchera, and, for a truly theatrical touch, the great floppy leaves of ruby chard on their blood red stems.

Rose (*Rosa* cv.)

PRIMARY COLORS

LEFT: Red nasturtiums scrambling over the wall continue the theme set by the dahlia 'Ellen Huston'. Another primary color, such as the blue agapanthus lily, makes a strong combination.

203

Nasturtium (*Tropaeolum majus*)

Lupin (*Lupinus* cv.)

Field poppy (*Papaver rhoeas*)

Jerusalem cross (*Lychnis chalcedonica*)

A silver edging of lamb's ears tempers a stand of late red dahlias and nicotiana.

Red Flowers

Scarlet tulips, poppies, dahlias – red flowers in the garden are a force to be reckoned with. Use them with passion and fervor, but keep them away from shy pastels, which will retire, shocked, into the background. Mix them with other hot colors for a warm, rich effect or throw in a touch of pure blue for an extra jolt.

Cool Borders

Sweet pea (*Lathyrus odoratus*)

Planting your garden with cool subtle shades at the boundaries is a clever trick that will make it seem larger, as the pale colors appear to blur into the landscape beyond. Pink and blue flowers with linking grey foliage make a gentle pastel color scheme, with an accent or two of white here and there to add some light.

For an enduring effect, choose a shrub with a long flowering season – a pink lavatera, or a panicle-flowered hydrangea – then add further tones of pink. Verbenas, monardas, penstemons, all come in shades of pink, but if you substitute another variety, the final effect will be quite different. *Perovskia atriplicifolia* will introduce an element of blue, which can be reinforced with agapanthus lilies or bristly anchusa.

Foliage is a vital part of a cool planting. The gray felted leaves of *Lychnis coronaria* 'Alba' fit perfectly, with the added advantage of the plant's white flowers, which will lighten the overall planting.

EASY ON THE EYE
ABOVE: *Pink and blue are an undemanding color combination, provided here by pink evening primrose and Texas bluebonnets.*

Pink-flowered sage (*Salvia officinalis* 'Rosea')

Columbine (*Aquilegia vulgaris*)

Lilac (*Syringa* cv.)

Hyacinth (*Hyacinthus* sp.)

ROSES AND DELPHINIUMS

RIGHT: Purple-blue spires of delphiniums tower above pink roses in a restful scheme highlighted by a pergola swathed in white rambling roses.

Phlox 'Chattahoochee'

Meadow rue
(*Thalictrum* sp.)

Deadnettle
(*Lamium maculatum*)

Clematis
(*Clematis* 'Arabella')

Ornamental onion
(*Allium aflatunense*)

Trachelium caeruleum

Blue and Purple Borders

Blue and purple are two of the most restful colors; they add a sense of calm and space to any composition. A bluebell wood in spring is filled with a blue haze that drifts between the trees like smoke. The same effect can be achieved in a garden by allowing blue and purple plants to self-seed, so that they form a sheen linking the entire planting.

A blue and purple scheme for the border could usefully include an early clematis such as *C. alpina* 'Frances Rivis' which is light blue, and carpets of toning purplish blue scilla and forget-me-nots. Inky blue irises, sky blue flax, and a bush of ceanothus continue the blue theme, which can be further enhanced by *Geranium* 'Johnson's Blue' and *Clematis* 'Jackmanii'. Mix in some hazy purple catmint and a dash of white roses for summer contrast. If you want to include foliage that contributes to a blue and purple border, look out for *Hosta sieboldiana* or *H.* 'Buckshaw Blue', or the glaucous-leaved rose *Rosa glauca*.

PURPLE PATCHES
RIGHT: Wine-dark purple lupins and salvia are complemented by an old-fashioned pink rose.

BLUE MOODS
BELOW: Unopened buds of delphinium 'Carl Topping' are distinctly blue, but the flowers in full bloom are violet hued.

A plethora of spring bedding plants in purple and contrasting colors.

Forget-me-not (*Myosotis*)

Iris sibirica 'Perry's Blue'

Geranium x *magnificum*

Agapanthus

Blue and Purple Flowers

Violet, mauve, and purple all have a common denominator: the color blue. Pale blue forget-me-nots can stand alone or create a background for showier species such as tulips and wallflowers. Summer blue flowers suffused with purple – irises, gorgeous agapanthus lilies, campanulas – complement each other if planted side by side, or benefit from a shot of yellow or orange to intensify their depth.

A SWATHE OF PINK

BELOW: This sea of poppies in varying strengths of pink all have sooty black stamens that add contrast close up.

Pink Borders

Pink is a gentle color that expresses itself in subtle associations, flushing the petals of apple blossom in spring and tinting the petals of white hydrangeas as they age. It is a vital component in the garden to soften the planting and create a relaxed effect. Pink is also a color of infinate variety, from the palest tints to the hottest hues.

Ring the changes in a sugar-pink border by dropping in a few accents of scorching magenta – alliums or lupins – or even a dash of bright red, which is, after all, just the brighter end of the spectrum. Later in the summer, introduce a few surprises with maroon-black hollyhocks or port-wine penstemons to spice up the border.

Look to the pink flowers themselves for a clue as to how to extend the color scheme. Some pink roses such as *Rosa gallica versicolor* 'Rosa Mundi' or *R.* 'Ferdinand Pichard' are striped with crimson and white, whose color can be echoed with white violas, crimson and white sweet Williams, and old-fashioned pinks with lacy patterns and fringed petals.

A PINK SPECTRUM

RIGHT: This stunning pink border uses elements from the entire color range, from purple-black hollyhocks to palest pink lavatera.

IN THE PINK

BELOW: Blowsy clumps of Phlox 'Franz Schubert' are glimpsed through a screen of closely packed flowerheads of Allium sphaerocephalon *and upright spikes of liatris.*

213

Phlox paniculata 'Eva Cullum'

The low-growing ground-cover rose 'The Fairy' tumbles over a border of deep pink *Heterocentron elegans*.

Double daisy (*Bellis perennis*)

Peony (*Paeonia suffruticosa*)

Primula abonica

Pink Flowers

Friendly shades of pink are easy on the eye and easy to place successfully in the garden. Choose species with added interest, such as white-centered double daisies, and mix pale pinks with zingy magenta and crimson to change the pace and intensity of the planting.

215

White Borders

A border full of white flowers will continue to glimmer in the last light of evening long after other colors have been reduced to an indecipherable thickening of darkness. White flowers look best accentuated by green foliage and nothing else. You can emphasize this combination of green and white by using variegated leaves. Try *Hosta fortunei* 'Albopicta' or *H.* 'Francee', the variegated *Iris pallida* 'Variegata' or *Cornus alba* 'Elegantissima'.

A white border in spring might begin with white narcissi, snowdrops, sweet woodruff, and white fritillaries and tulips. In summer white peonies, roses, goat's rue, Madonna lilies, and foxgloves will fit the bill.

Keep all your whites within the same tone. Different hints of other colors can creep into a surprising number of white flowers. If you mix a creamy rose with pinkish white poppies, the outcome will be different from the planned effect of a pure white border.

WHITE ON WHITE
LEFT: *Even the white-painted clapboard walls contribute to a color scheme of white rambling roses and daisies.*

PURE AS THE DRIVEN SNOW
OPPOSITE: *This white spring border is complemented by variegated foliage.*

Tulip (*Tulipa* cv.)

A bright cheerful spring border shows the elegance of white blooms and green foliage.

Iceberg rose (*Rosa* 'Iceberg')

Anemone x *hybrida* 'Honorine Jobert'

Celmisia hookeri

GARDENER'S CHOICE

White Flowers

Most species have at some time been bred to create a white variety to satisfy the demands of the many gardeners who want to make a white border. There are white roses, delphiniums, daisies, foxgloves, and many, many more to choose from.

White flowers are also extremely useful for separating clashing colors within a border, so that you can create some interesting effects without assaulting the senses too violently.

Hollyhock (*Alcea rosea*)

219

Green Borders

There are so many shades of green that it is well worth cultivating a green border. They rely heavily on texture and shape for effect. Architectural plants with sufficient impact to stop you in your tracks are essential – bear's breeches, spurges, or a stand of finely divided fennel fronds. It is also a place to show off curiosities such as green-flowered *Nicotiana* 'Lime Green', *Fritillaria pontica*, *Smyrnium perfoliatum*, and the more commonly grown species such as lady's mantle, *Tellima grandiflora*, and astrantia. For the truly dedicated colorist, there is even a green rose: *R.* x *odorata* 'Viridiflora'.

There is something very restful about a soothing green foliage garden. It gives you the freedom to examine leaves in all their myriad forms and shades of green without the distraction of showy flowers, and the chance to admire the delicate fronds of ferns, narrow-leaved grasses, the coarse-lobed leaves of *Rodgersia aesculifolia* and the shiny, light-reflecting leaves of holly or laurel.

Guelder rose
(*Viburnum opulus*)

A CONTEMPORARY PLANTING

LEFT: *The clean lines of this modern garden rely mostly on the varied effects of different foliage, including pittosporum, phormium, and grasses.*

A WOODLAND GARDEN

RIGHT: *Shade-loving plants – ferns, hostas, bergenia, and Solomon's seal – demonstrate the vast difference in greens and in the form of the leaves themselves.*

Euphorbia characias ssp. *wulfenii* underplants a cream rose in this stylish planting.

Fritillaria verticillata

Lady's mantle (*Alchemilla mollis*)

Bells of Ireland (*Moluccella laevis*)

Euphorbia characias ssp. *wulfenii*

Green Flowers

Green flowers can be used to subtle effect to introduce wonderfully varied shades of green and some curiously different flower shapes to your garden – bottlebrush euphorbias, tiny starry lady's mantle, and the strangely sculptural bells of Ireland.

Garden Style

Choosing a Style

A garden is a very personal place and should include all the ingredients that you like best – a tangle of roses, a pool to muse by, a knot garden of clipped box. Don't let fashion dictate your choice: design your garden to suit you.

AT THE WATER'S EDGE

A densely planted poolside, and a seat from which to admire it (left), *are two of the garden's greatest pleasures. Elegant irises* (above) *thrive on the wet margins of the pond.*

Informal Style

The best-known example of informal planting is the cottage garden, where flowers compete for space and attention with seemingly minimum intervention. However, even the most random-seeming array of plants needs some kind of order. The key to success is to make sure there is an underlying structure before you begin to add the plants. A ground plan will allocate each plant its place and prevent a charming profusion from descending into chaos.

An informal garden can be more difficult to design than a formal one. Its nature precludes the use of straight edges or geometric shapes to define different areas and instead lawns, flower beds, paths, and borders must take the form of fluid shapes, free-form lines and interlocking curves.

Paths, pergolas, fences, and trellises all help to give the garden a sense of purpose, and any hard landscaping is soon rendered unobtrusive as the plants become established.

Low-growing plants at the edges of borders soon spill over onto paths, blurring any harsh edges and disguising the man-made elements beneath. Species that self-seed prolifically, such as the ever-popular lady's mantle and feverfew, are particularly welcome, as they quickly colonize bare stone patios and too-pristine gravel paths.

Purple foxglove
(*Digitalis purpurea*)

A COUNTRY GARDEN

LEFT: *In this traditional cottage garden, tall plants spring up amongst low-growing species with scant regard for the classic rules of planning a border.*

229

Purely decorative features can strike a discordant note in an informal garden. Paired tubs of lollipop-shaped bay trees will definitely look out of place in a cottage-style setting, as will symmetrical arrangements of standard roses or fuchsias. Instead, make sure that any features perform a useful function – a wigwam of canes for sweet peas to scramble up, a rustic arch to support roses or clematis, or a tub of lilies that can be moved around to bring scent and color to a shady corner.

A SPLASH OF COLOR

ABOVE: *Variegated ivy and intense purple verbena bring color and interest to a dull corner.*

WALL DRESSING

RIGHT: *Wall-mounted containers, such as this elegant head planted with variegated pelargoniums, add variety at a higher level.*

A RIOT OF COLOR

OPPOSITE: *An unrestrained mixture of humble marigolds and hebes creates a stunning contrast to a smoothly mown lawn.*

Formal Style

Formal garden designs have an impeccable pedigree that stretches back generations. From the strictly symmetrical garden plans of villas in ancient Rome to the intricate Elizabethan knot gardens and the great gardens at Versailles, the stunning visual nature of these gardens has made them enduringly popular.

Knot gardens and parterres must be clipped and weeded regularly to keep their crisp outlines, but the result makes all the effort worthwhile. Shapes and beds are defined by numerous small paths that not only lay the basis for the design, but are extremely practical too, as every corner of the flower beds can be reached without stepping onto the soil. Edging for the beds is essential, whether it's a living border of tightly clipped box or cotton lavender, or a retaining rim of timber, brick, or terracotta tiles.

A HINT OF FORMALITY

ABOVE: All the elements of a formal garden are here, yet the wayward spires of the foxgloves stop the overall effect from being too fussy and precise.

CIRCLES WITHIN CIRCLES

RIGHT: The layout of this rose garden is based on concentric circles of clipped box, focusing the view inward onto a central statue.

A CLEAR REFLECTION
ABOVE: The center of this geometric pool is kept entirely free of plants for enhanced simplicity.

Filling the beds with flowers from a restricted color palette, perhaps silver or white, will reinforce the formal theme; while a more casual effect can be achieved by using a rainbow of colors and spreading species to contrast with the rigid enclosures.

A formal design lends itself to almost any situation. As well as being ideally suited to a large plot, a simple geometric design translates brilliantly to a tiny modern garden and creates a classic, elegant effect where space is limited.

MIRROR IMAGES

ABOVE: *This formal garden enclosed by a tall yew hedge relies on absolute symmetry for effect, using repeated tubs of marguerites and box topiary.*

DESIGNS IN GREENERY

RIGHT: *This modern reinterpretation of a traditional parterre has eschewed flowers for greenery and relies on pattern and precision for interest.*

Lawns

A velvety, well-kept lawn makes an elegant focal point for any garden and creates an attractive contrast to the array of textures and colors to be found in beds and borders. As well as being easy on the eye, the lawn is an incredibly versatile area, providing the perfect spot in which to sit and enjoy your garden.

A lawn is also an ideal area for children to play on, and is essential under swings and climbing frames to cushion inevitable tumbles. If you are planting a lawn for this purpose, choose a seed mix of tough, durable species that will withstand the rough and tumble of family life.

Lawns respond well to a little care and attention. If you feed, weed, and mow your lawn regularly it will repay you by becoming a lush, green oasis that will give you pleasure and service for many years to come.

SMOOTH CONTRAST

BELOW: This smooth lawn makes an ideal backdrop for the mature borders of this large garden. Wide sweeping curves look good and are easier to mow than narrow strips of lawn.

SMALL BUT BEAUTIFUL
LEFT: *Making the lawn circular draws the eye out to the boundaries of the garden and makes this small yard appear wider.*

Repairing a lawn edge

Sections of established turf can easily be cut out of the lawn and lifted to make any necessary repairs to damaged areas. A well-worn lawn edge can be remedied by simply cutting out the piece of turf with the battered border and turning it around so that the damaged area lies within the lawn. The neat, grass edge is restored and the damaged section of the lawn can be quickly and easily repaired.

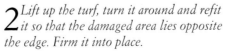

1 *Cut a section of turf big enough to include the damaged edge, slicing through the root system of the grass.*

2 *Lift up the turf, turn it around and refit it so that the damaged area lies opposite the edge. Firm it into place.*

3 *Make up the damaged area with a little fine soil sown with grass seed, which should start to grow within two weeks.*

A Profusion of Flowers

For many gardeners, flowers are the primary reason for cultivating their plot. From the very first snowdrops emerging from a blanket of snow to the last late-flowering Michaelmas daisies, with a little forward planning it is possible to put on a massed display of blooms throughout the year.

As carpets of spring-flowering bulbs begin to fade, a wave of perennials is waiting in the wings to take their place, with any conspicuous gaps filled by pretty summer annuals such as clarkia, nigella, and marigolds. As summer blazes on, lilies unfurl and roses drop their petals, to be superceded by feathery golden rod, brash yellow coneflowers, and delicate fall crocuses. Even in the depths of winter a garden can produce a small nosegay: Christmas roses, sprays of winter jasmine, wintersweet, and the odd late rosebud. A plethora of flowers can lift the spirits and awaken the senses, so let your garden bloom and bring a riot of color into your life.

A PRETTY POSY

ABOVE: This cheerful posy picked from a summer garden is a combination of the exotic and the everyday. Glory lilies, pink lilies, and marigolds make ideal cut flowers.

SUMMER EXUBERANCE

RIGHT: Marguerites, pelargoniums, nasturtiums, and petunias have practically engulfed this garden seat in a wild embrace.

HEADY MIXTURE

ABOVE: *Permanent plantings of roses, irises, geums, and agapanthus lilies are boosted with an explosion of colorful annuals – antirrhinums, marigolds, and nigella.*

A SPRING CARPET

RIGHT: *This tapestry of colors on a spring rockery is created with a combination of alpine plants and bulbs – tulips, hyacinths, grape hyacinths, and winter pansies.*

Water Features

Water lily (*Nymphaea* sp.)

Water has long been considered an essential element of garden design. It can animate a garden with sound or movement, or create a quiet corner for contemplation. Even in the smallest space, a simple pool can open up the garden by introducing areas of clear water without too much loss of ground.

The soothing splash and trickle of a fountain is one of the most relaxing sounds in the garden and can actually help screen out intrusive traffic noise by focusing your attention on its own sound. It needn't be an elaborate affair: a simple wall-mounted mask can endlessly spout water into a small basin with a concealed pump to recycle the water.

Building a pond in your garden is also a guaranteed way to attract wildlife, with frogs and newts making their way to it when it is barely finished. It will also vastly extend the range of plants you are able to grow. Dwarf water lilies and other aquatic species will even grow happily in a half-barrel of water if they are thinned from time to time.

PERPETUAL MOTION

LEFT: *Even the smallest garden has room for a fountain. As well as being an attractive addition to the garden, a wall-mounted reservoir poses no risk to children.*

A PERFECT POOL

RIGHT: *A large informal pool fed by a small waterfall combines reflective still waters with a gentle background trickle.*

Hidden Retreats

In a busy world, moments of privacy are priceless. Everyone dreams of a secluded haven to call their own and, even in a city where every open space is overlooked by windows on all sides, it is possible to create a truly secluded spot.

Plants can be used as living screens, both to block ugly views and to counter prying eyes. Trellises are easy to install and can be planted with clematis, honeysuckle, and jasmine or even fast-growing annuals, such as the cup-and-saucer vine, for rapid results. Small trees such as the variegated maple or shrubs like the golden-leaved variety of Mexican orange blossom grow quite happily in tubs and can be moved as needed to enclose intimate areas for sitting and reading.

Even though an urban garden may be small, don't be tempted to scale down the planting – dense bushy shrubs, tall bamboos and vigorous climbing plants all give valuable cover and a sense of seclusion. Another trick to block out the outside world is to make an internal focus for the garden: a bold statue, a fountain or small pool – anything that draws the eye away from external distractions. A secluded spot will provide you with a sanctuary from the cares of the world, and will help to make your garden a truly unique place.

URBAN RETREAT

LEFT: *Lush planting with plenty of height from a tall bamboo forms a secluded area for sitting out.*

UP ON THE ROOF

RIGHT: *Roof gardens are exposed to extremes of weather, but in this elegant dining room high above the city streets, trellising acts as a windbreak for both people and plants.*

Outdoor Dining

One of the greatest pleasures of having a garden is being able to eat outside and it makes sense to choose a permanent spot for your outdoor dining room. Ideally, it will be sunny but with some protection from the fierce midday sun; sheltered from prevailing wind, but not too shady; and not too far from the house to make fetching forgotten items too tedious to contemplate.

A parasol can compensate for lack of shade, but for a more permanent solution, train a grape vine over a pergola in the tradition of Greek tavernas. Your site should also be flat, preferably paved, so that chairs and tables won't wobble or tilt. Whatever you choose, an outdoor dining room is a pleasurable place to while away the warm days and evenings.

A SHELTERED SPOT

LEFT: *Climbing plants on an overhead pergola cast a gentle dappled shade on the dining table, with a parasol to provide extra protection at midday.*

ALFRESCO DINING

BELOW LEFT: *A sturdy mosaic table laid with the makings of a summer lunch is drawn up against the shelter of the garden wall.*

A SEA VIEW

RIGHT: *In this idyllic location, a raised deck has been built to take maximum advantage of the view.*

A MINIMALIST HAVEN

LEFT: *An expanse of pale wooden decking and limited planting are the perfect uncluttered antidote to the stresses of city life.*

POOLSIDE PARADISE

RIGHT: *These garden chairs are positioned for contemplation of an azure pool. There are no hard lines here, even the steps are softly clad in ivy.*

LOUNGING AROUND

BELOW: *These reclining chairs are placed to watch the sunset over the city, set against an elegant background of creepers and unobtrusive gray trellis.*

Somewhere to Relax

Gardening isn't all hard work. When planning the basic design, be sure to include a vantage point where you can sit back and contemplate the view. Whether this is a vast panorama or a flower-crammed backyard, there will always be something to look at. Sitting and relaxing takes on a whole new dimension when the natural drama of the garden is unfolding in front of you.

Take your lifestyle into account. If you are an early riser, position a bench where it will catch the morning sun; if you are out all day, you'll want a seat where you can watch the sun set. Move a garden chair around to suit your mood: beside the pond to watch dragonflies skimming over the water; under a silver birch to appreciate a breeze rustling the leaves. Make sure there are fragrant plants close by – there is nothing like the scent of lavender or jasmine's heady perfume to lift your spirits.

The Garden Framework

Paths, steps, fences, arches, and walls all form the bones of a garden. This hard landscaping must be finished before planting can begin. Once the framework is established, everything else will fall naturally into place.

SIZZLING COLOR

A trellis takes on a new dimension when clad in a vibrant plant such as bougainvillea (left). Hollyhocks (above) add height and color to an informal setting.

Large Gardens

A large garden has enormous potential; the only difficulty lies in deciding where to begin. One option is to organize it into more manageable areas by creating gardens within a garden. Dividing a garden into outdoor 'rooms', each with a different style of planting, has long been a popular way of coping with large expanses of land. Hedges, fences, or other boundaries can be used to enclose different areas and will contribute valuable structure in winter, when the bones of the design are laid bare.

Alternatively, you can opt for the opposite extreme and turn the garden into a vast landscape that looks natural but is entirely man-made. You could incorporate dramatic water features, such as a tumbling waterfall, or even a fake ruin in the style of the great romantic landscape gardeners of the eighteenth century.

A garden of reasonable size will have a variety of micro-climates – shady spots, open windy sites, dry areas, patches of wetland – giving you the opportunity to plant some very

SWEETLY SCENTED
ABOVE: Roses and lavender make perfect planting partners.

FORMING A LINK
OPPOSITE: A small wooden bridge and a series of stepping stones lead from the open landscape to a more intimate seating area.

ROOM TO BREATHE
LEFT: With plenty of space, deep borders give plants room to grow into generous clumps and drifts. This site has the luxury of its own kitchen garden beyond the herbaceous borders.

different species. Trees play a big role in a large garden. If you are prepared to wait a few years for the results, you could even create your own woodland.

In a rural setting, a garden should show off the landscape visible beyond the boundaries to its best advantage. Use arches or tunnels of trees to frame a view, keeping nearby colors muted so as not to detract from it. Where the garden meets open countryside, planting a wildflower meadow will help blur the boundaries between the cultivated and the wild.

ENCLOSED GRANDEUR

LEFT: *An elevated view illustrates how well-trimmed yew hedges divide this garden into outdoor rooms and have a restraining influence on the profuse planting.*

A CASCADE OF COLOR

RIGHT: *This rustic bench is an ideal vantage point to enjoy a densely planted and textured slope, kept in place by a retaining wall.*

FOCAL POINTS

RIGHT: *In a large garden, a decorative summerhouse, statues, and carefully sited urns all act as focal points within the wider view.*

Small Spaces

Even a small area of lawn or a yard can be converted into a delightful garden. Think carefully about your choice of plants, as in a small space they have to work harder than their counterparts in a bigger garden. When there's no space to shift the focus to different areas for each season, every plant has to contribute something to the planting scheme all year round. Evergreens are an obvious choice, plus shrubs that have colorful foliage in the fall, or bright bare stems in winter.

When space is at a premium, think vertically and use creepers to cover your walls. Choose a few clematis carefully and you can have a glorious display of flowers from spring right through to fall. Ivy is an evergreen favorite, while the climbing *Hydrangea anomala* subsp. *petiolaris* will tolerate, or even thrive on, shady walls. For a cascade of summer color, why not grow an array of cheerful pelargoniums, pansies, and busy-lizzies in wall-mounted pots or hanging baskets?

PERFECTLY FORMED

RIGHT: This well-designed garden has all the traditional elements of a much larger space – lawns, borders, urns, topiary – without feeling overcrowded.

GARDEN IN MINIATURE

BELOW: Even a narrow balcony has room for tubs of color – white magnolia and a scarlet camellia.

THINKING VERTICALLY

ABOVE: Trellis secured to a high wall makes fixing pots easier, and raises the plants to receive the sunlight.

Regal pelargonium
(*Pelargonium*)

Don't be afraid to use bold features such as an over-sized urn or a dramatic statue on a plinth. A large urn gives the impression of a garden on a grand scale. It may help to think of your garden as a stage set, with 'props' that can be moved around or changed entirely to modify the emphasis.

Using pots is the perfect way to add seasonal flowers to a small garden, replanting them with spring bulbs, annual bedding, or summer-flowering lilies, and moving them around to introduce color and contrast as needed.

RAMBLING ROSES

ABOVE: In a patio garden there is no room for traditional borders, but roses growing over an arch and walls more than compensate.

YEAR-ROUND GREENERY

RIGHT: A permanent evergreen framework is vital even on the smallest scale.

A BRICK TERRACE
LEFT: *A little enclosed garden paved with attractive bricks leads to a raised wooden deck, signalling the approach to the house.*

REPEATING PATTERN
RIGHT: *The design of the brick-built raised beds is repeated in the brick edging of the stone steps for a coordinated look in an urban garden.*

UNDER A CANOPY OF CLEMATIS
BELOW LEFT: *Stone slabs form a stable base for a wrought-iron garden bench but a luscious canopy of* Clematis montana *and laburnum dispels any hard-edged notions.*

Paved Areas

In heavily used areas of the garden, it is essential to have a durable surface under foot. A proper patio for dining out means you don't have to worry about chairs sinking into the lawn or getting muddy feet.

All-over paving is also a good practical option in a small backyard. Lay it on a proper foundation of hardcore topped with a bed of sand for long-lasting stability. Brushing in a little extra sand between the gaps should be sufficient to point the paving, particularly if you want plants to seed in the gaps.

Your choice of paving should be influenced by two factors – traditional regional materials, and your budget. Genuine local stone looks extremely attractive but may be expensive. Luckily there are some convincing reconstituted stones on the market, which may be encouraged to mellow and age more quickly by painting them with yogurt or liquid manure.

Bricks can be laid in attractive patterns to form a terrace or patio. Always use proper paving bricks as house bricks will succumb to frost and water damage. Remember that many plants will grow in paving if given space to establish.

SOFT EDGES

BELOW: Opportunistic self-seeders such as lady's mantle soon colonize even the smallest gaps and help to blur any hard edges.

If you are making a paved area next to the house, match the tone of the paviors to the house bricks for a harmonious effect. Leaving gaps between the paved area and the house will allow plants and shrubs to be grown to soften stark edges. Where paving butts up to the walls of the house, be careful not to cover the damp-proof course and make sure the patio slopes gently away from the house to avoid flooding the foundations in heavy rain.

CRAZY PAVING

LEFT: *A random mix of brick, stone, and colored tiles continues the theme set by the garden's purple and blue painted walls.*

Planting in paving

With a little time, a bare paved area will be colonized by self-sown species from within the garden. To help things along you can also sow seed directly into the gaps between slabs. This will soften the appearance of your hard edges, and is a good opportunity to introduce some new plants. Corsican mint and Welsh poppy will grow in shadier spots, while creeping thyme grows happily in full sun. Heartsease will tolerate either condition.

1 *Clear the gaps between slabs using a chisel and mallet, then brush away any loose material.*

2 *Fill the space with a soil-based compost, sprinkling and pushing it in by hand. Sow the seed directly into the gaps.*

3 *Cover the seeds with more compost. Once the seedlings have germinated, water them in dry weather and thin them out as necessary.*

Pinks (*Dianthus* cv)

Golden thyme (*Thymus* x
citriodorus 'Aureus')

Bugle (*Ajuga reptans*)

Even paved areas can make a colorful contribution.

Plants for Paving

Plants can help integrate hard surfaces into the rest of the garden either by growing in the gaps between paving or by spilling over from adjoining flower beds. Encourage herbs such as thyme, Corsican mint, and lawn chamomile to grow between stones. They release a delicious scent when crushed. Ground-cover plants such as bugle, violets, and pinks will disguise hard edges.

Sweet violet (*Viola odorata*)

263

Paths

Paths ease your way around the garden and help to protect its more delicate parts. They also play an interesting visual role in the overall design. Consider whether your garden is formal or relaxed and create a path that suits your style.

You can use a variety of materials to create a path including paving slabs, decking, or even grass, but the easiest way is to use gravel or shingle. If the route is well trodden, it can be spread straight onto the ground with a simple timber edge. Gravel is ideal for curved paths, or make a traditional brick border by digging a shallow trench either side of the path and putting in the bricks at an angle. To make a straight gravel path more interesting, site bushy sprawling plants close to the edge that will narrow the width as they grow.

Brick paths may be laid in traditional herringbone or basketweave patterns. If the ground is firm, lay them on a bed of sand between timber edges. On soft or recently disturbed ground, make a hardcore base below the sand.

GRASSY AVENUE

TOP LEFT: *Grass paths are ideal for areas of the garden that are not heavily used. This woodland path is bordered with bluebells in spring.*

A WORK OF ART

BELOW LEFT: *Pebbles in contrasting colors have been painstakingly set in concrete to form a mosaic path of elegant curlicues.*

SINUOUS PATH

RIGHT: *Gravel and shingle are the best choice for a complexly curved path.*

HIDDEN TRACKS

BELOW: *A narrow brick path that has all but disappeared under encroaching plants forces you to walk slowly and appreciate the garden.*

265

Gates

Historically, one of the main functions of a gate was to impress visitors, as well as providing access. These days, a gate can be used as an extension of the garden, providing a perfect excuse to introduce a romantic entrance.

A gate to the front garden should echo the front door, taking into account the overall architecture of the house. Wooden picket gates tend to suit older properties and can also be used in a suburban setting; five-bar gates are strictly rural and look out of place in town.

Metal gates are strong and sturdy, and an open design in wrought iron is secure without being oppressive. If it seems rather hard in appearance, why not train honeysuckle or clematis from an adjoining fence or wall through into the gate itself? The stems are flexible enough to allow the gate to open and close gently and will soften the appearance of the entrance.

A gateway from one area of the garden to another can be just a gap in a hedge or an open archway. Alternatively, why not use a gateway to frame a tantalizing view?

UP THE GARDEN PATH

ABOVE: A simple painted wooden gate flanked by rustic stone pillars opens onto a no-nonsense path leading straight to the front door.

SWEETLY FRAMED IN FLOWERS

RIGHT: In a more formal setting, the curve of an Arts-and-Crafts-style gate echoes the overhead arch, almost hidden by a flourish of clematis and roses.

A WELCOMING SIGHT

LEFT AND FAR LEFT: Clematis are ideal climbing plants to train over a gateway: they are not too heavy or rampantly vigorous, and their simple flowers will charm visitors.

Arches and Pergolas

An arch or a pergola, swathed in roses or clad in clematis can be one of a garden's most romantic features. You can make the structures as functional or as decorative as you like.

A pergola above a paved patio will provide privacy from overlooking buildings and valuable shade at the height of summer. In a small backyard, a pergola attached to the house links building and garden, and makes the space feel contained and comfortable.

An arch may be used simply as a structure to support climbing plants, or to frame a view or a focal point or link two areas. In a rustic garden, it need be no more than a few stripped hazel poles, bent over and secured in the earth. Plant them with sweet peas, canary creeper, morning glory, or other annual climbers, as such a structure will have only a limited lifespan. In a formal setting, a wrought-iron arch is more appropriate, perhaps with an elegant finial set on an ogee top.

Rose (*Rosa* 'Gloire de Dijon')

A COVERED ENTRANCE

LEFT: A small home-made wooden pergola planted with Clematis *'Jackmanii' leads from the garden to the house.*

A SECRET BOWER

LEFT: *An informal pointed trellis-work arch, clad with Rosa 'Madame Caroline Testout' is surrounded by a sea of herbaceous planting.*

ROMANTIC ROSES

BELOW: *A wide metal arch covered in climbing roses is the perfect ingredient for a romantic garden.*

SCENTED SHADE

RIGHT: *Rambling roses
'Adélaïde d'Orléans' and
'Auguste Gervais' perfume
the air and make this
pergola-covered patio a
heavenly spot in which to
sit and dream.*

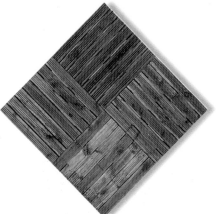

KEEP IT SIMPLE

ABOVE: Many garden centers sell decking in ready-made treated sections.

Decking

Wooden decking is an alternative to paving and another way of creating an all-weather surface. It is much warmer underfoot than stone and a lot more versatile, especially for structures raised above ground, such as a sun deck or balcony. It blends perfectly with weatherboarded houses and is particularly appropriate for a seaside garden, with its visual references to jetties and boardwalks. Where decking is laid at ground level it pays to raise it off the earth a little or to lay it on a bed of gravel. This allows water to drain off and air to circulate, reducing the wood's tendency to rot.

Hardwood decking needs no special treatment and will weather to an understated silvery finish. Treated softwoods are less inherently attractive but will take colored wood stains readily, which means you can even tint the decking to suit an outdoor color scheme.

Decking is ideal for roof gardens. Not only is it attractive, it has many other advantages. It helps distribute the weight of container-grown shrubs and trees, and raised beds, so protecting the roof from damage. It also lets rainwater drain away easily.

DECKED IN FINERY
LEFT: *A streamlined wooden deck suits the clean lines of a modern building. Decking is relatively easy to manipulate to accommodate an obstacle such as a tree growing close to the house.*

ON THE WATERFRONT
RIGHT: *A wooden deck is the natural choice for a tranquil poolside terrace.*

Building your own raised deck

If you have room for only a small area of decking, why not build your own? Making your own deck is not too difficult and is considerably less expensive than one that is professionally built. Making it yourself gives you total control over your choice of materials and is also extremely satisfying. To help protect the joists from rot, raise them above the soil by laying them across a system of bricks placed on concrete pads.

1 Space concrete pads about 3 ft (1 m) apart, using four for each section of decking. Top each one with a brick.

2 Lay timber joists on the bricks and lay rafters across at right angles. Fix them in position with nails or screws.

3 Lay the planks so that they run in the same direction as the joists and fix them down with galvanized nails.

4 Conceal the joists and bases with vertical boarding nailed to the ends of the joists.

Steps

Creating a change of level in your garden adds interest and prevents the garden from looking boring when seen as a whole. Steps look wonderful decorated with a simple but colorful array of pots, or with generous plantings that spill over onto the edges. Place pots on each step to herald your ascent.

While a flight of steps is innately functional, it can also be a decorative element in its own right. Shallow steps can look extremely elegant in a broad flight punctuating a low bank or wall – a semi-circular arrangement creates an effect that is even more theatrical.

The flat surface of each step is known as the tread, and the vertical height as the riser. The golden rule for creating a comfortable – and safe – flight of steps is that the deeper the tread, the shallower the riser should be. Even when steps are built from irregular materials such as rough-hewn rocks or logs, it is essential to keep the same proportions throughout the flight for safety's sake.

STEPS AS A FOCAL POINT

OPPOSITE: Making the steps broad and adding a defining pergola makes a feature from the change of level.

PLAIN AND SIMPLE

ABOVE LEFT: Graphic unadorned steps lead to a terrace paved in the same material for a sense of continuity. A collection of containers stops the overall effect from being too angular.

SLOWLY ASCENDING

ABOVE RIGHT: Wooden risers and gravel treads suit a set of shallow steps in a rural plot. The steps' proportions dictate a leisurely pace through the garden.

THE GARDEN FRAMEWORK

WITHIN THESE WALLS

OPPOSITE: Californian lilac benefits from a supporting wall. As well as needing deep foundations, a wall of this height has reinforcing buttresses for additional safety.

THE PERFECT BACKDROP

RIGHT: Wisteria will flourish against a warm wall. Some specimens can live for a hundred years and grow very heavy, so fix wall-trained plants firmly.

Tree ivy (*Hedera helix* 'Arborescens')

Walls

A walled garden is highly prized. Within its shelter it is possible to grow tender plants successfully, to train fruit trees such as peaches and apricots on sheltered, sunny walls, and, on a more fanciful note, to create a truly secret garden totally hidden from passers-by.

Make the most of your walls if you have them. They add height to the garden and provide a sheltered backdrop for spires of tall plants, such as hollyhocks and delphiniums, and provide a framework for climbing plants. Over the years, stone walls can become colonized with plants to form a sheer rock garden.

When choosing your plants for a walled site, take into account how much shade the wall casts and remember that soil tends to be dry at the base. Even the walls of your house can be clothed in plants. Wisteria and ivy add a traditional feel.

THE GARDEN FRAMEWORK

The expense of building a wall, whether from brick or stone, means that you are unlikely to tear down existing fences or hedges and enclose your garden with brand new walls. Instead, think of more modest ways to use them: to retain earth at the bottom of a sloping bed, to build a raised bed, or use low walls to flank a flight of steps.

A WALL GARDEN

RIGHT: *Stonecrop has naturalized in a mellow brick wall.*

IN THE SHELTER OF THE WALL

OPPOSITE: *This weathered brick and flint wall encloses a host of colorful cottage-garden annuals, including cosmos, antirrhinums, and golden rod.*

THE ART OF CAMOUFLAGE

BELOW: *At the back of the border a pyracantha has been coaxed into a fan to disguise a worn and patched brick wall.*

Planting in a wall

Many plants will readily self-seed and grow naturally in a wall as their common names imply – wallflowers, stonecrop, and rock rose. To exercise a little more choice in the matter, you can also introduce plants such as aubrieta and suitable alpines.

Walls made of brick are the most suitable for introducing new plants. Create a small crevice by chipping away the mortar.

1 *Using a moist clay-based soil, push as much as you can into a suitable crevice, leaving room for the plant's roots.*

2 *Holding the plant upright, push it into the crevice. Add more soil, firming it around the roots to cover them and hold the plant securely.*

Hedges

Hedges are obligingly flexible boundary plants. As well as defining the limits of your plot, they can form a backdrop for a border and act as a windbreak to protect less robust plants; they can screen buildings and even filter out noise.

A plain single-species hedge is best for a boundary, screen, or backdrop – yew, Western red cedar, hornbeam, or beech are ideal; other suitable plants are shown below. Shape it so it is wider at the base and narrower at the top: then it will withstand snowfall and let rain get to the roots. Where security is important, a hedge of prickly holly, hawthorn, or thorny hedging roses is a forceful deterrent.

Low hedging plants such as box and cotton lavender are traditionally used as edging in knot gardens and parterres.

Mahonia (*Mahonia* x *media*)

Western red cedar (*Thuja plicata*)

Yew (*Taxus baccata*)

SHELTER BELT

LEFT: *The annual climber, Flame nasturtium adds a dramatic splash of scarlet to a deep green yew hedge that protects the garden.*

NEATLY BORDERED

RIGHT: *A low box hedge in a formal garden encloses a rose bed.*

Hornbeam (*Carpinus betulus*)

Box (*Buxus sempervirens*)

Oval-leaved privet (*Ligustrum ovalifolium*)

Elaeagnus (*Elaeagnus* x *ebbingei*)

Fences and Dividers

Putting up a fence is the quickest way of enclosing a garden, and will give the same degree of privacy as a wall for a fraction of the cost. Many different styles of fence exist. In towns, close-boarded fences give maximum privacy and security. In a rural setting, a post and rail fence will keep out cattle and sheep without spoiling the view.

A pretty picket fence painted white and backed with roses and clematis suits a cottage garden, as would an informal fence built of hurdles – panels of woven willow or hazel. They look charmingly rustic and are good in windy sites where a more solid fence could blow down. Metal railings are appropriate for a town front garden or the grander country garden.

In a small garden a fence can be a better option than a hedge, which depletes the surrounding soil of nutrients and water and so deprives neighboring plants.

HOPS AND POLES

ABOVE: *Golden hop winds through a softly weathered paling fence, whose strong structural lines will be revealed when the hop dies back in winter.*

A DECORATIVE EXTENSION

RIGHT: *Attaching a trellis extension to a fence or wall is an easy and relatively cheap way of increasing privacy.*

Trellises

Decorative trellises have been used in gardens for centuries, to provide support for climbing plants, and to screen or divide different areas, increasing privacy without casting a great deal of shade. Trellis is ideal for a roof garden as it is lightweight and easy to fix and its open structure filters the wind, rather than blocks it, so avoiding wind turbulence in the very area that you are trying to protect.

Painting a trellis dark green will make it almost disappear into the surrounding greenery, and used as a divider, its open structure gives tantalizing glimpses of what lies beyond. Rustic arches can be built from trellis to make a feature of a climbing rose or clematis, and trellis panels can be fixed directly onto walls or fences to support climbing plants where they might not otherwise get a foothold.

A SUPPORTIVE SCREEN
OPPOSITE: Dual-purpose closed trellis set in a durable framework screens out an unwelcome view and provides a backdrop for the roses.

ON A SMALL SCALE
ABOVE: Trellis at its simplest, used to support a potted plant – a climbing grape ivy.

UNSEEN SUPPORT
LEFT: A sturdy frame is needed to support these swathes of bougainvillea.

A climbing rose creates a romantic backdrop.

Parthenocissus henryana

Honeysuckle (*Lonicera periclymenum* 'Belgica')

Solanum crispum 'Glasnevin'

Passion flower (*Passiflora caerulea*)

Climbing Plants

Climbing plants will soften a wall or fence, and give the garden height and perspective. Plant wooden obelisks and trellis arches with lighter species, such as sweet peas and morning glory; an old, more solid wall can support a heavyweight like wisteria.

For variety, choose a mixture of evergreen and deciduous climbers; and grow honeysuckle and passion flower for their blooms. Remember that some climbers, such as rambling roses and wisteria, need tying in.

Raised Beds

In gardens without soil, such as roof gardens or courtyards, raised beds are a good way to introduce more permanent planting than by simply relying on containers. They can be used to break up a large expanse of concrete or a patio, and to create different levels.

Brick-built beds with clean lines suit a more formal setting; in a rustic garden, pressure-treated logs can be laid and nailed together to make the beds. Alternatively, old railway sleepers can be used as retaining edges.

By filling the beds with the appropriate soil, you can also grow plants that might not otherwise thrive in the earth found naturally in your garden – acid-loving camellias and heathers, or alpines that need a free-draining gravelly soil. Include some plants with a trailing habit, to blur hard edges and emphasize the bed's height.

SPLIT-LEVEL PLANTING

ABOVE: This multi-level garden of tiered brick-built beds has increased the space available for planting.

STREAMLINED SIMPLICITY

OPPOSITE: A plain concrete raised border has been painted to match its surroundings and planted with simple, but shapely architectural species in a modern Californian roof garden.

Building a raised bed

A raised bed, whether built as a retaining wall or freestanding, is extremely useful in any garden. If you want to build a solid raised bed, start by making the footings. They should be slightly wider than the finished wall and about 12 in (30 cm) deep for stability. A coping of bricks laid lengthways across the wall gives a neat and weatherproof finish. Once the structure is complete, fill the base with stones or another drainage material.

1 *Mark out the bed with canes and string. Dig a trench for the footings, fill it with concrete and leave to set overnight.*

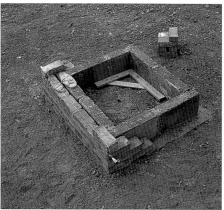

2 *Build an inner wall of cinder blocks cemented with mortar. Build the corners of the outer brick wall first, then fill in the rest.*

3 *Finish the bed with a brick coping laid across both walls. Place drainage material in the base of the bed, then fill with good quality topsoil.*

Perfect Planting

Think of trees and shrubs as forming the permanent structure of your garden, then add herbaceous perennials, summer annuals, bulbs, even ornamental grasses, for a palette of color and contrast.

SPECTACULAR SHRUBBERY

A border created entirely from shrubs (left) demonstrates their vast range of form. Lacecap hydrangeas (above) are perfect plants for adding color to a shrubbery.

RAISING PERSPECTIVE

*ABOVE: A sea of pink and purple flowers
is elevated to an eye-catching height by
a sturdy stone plinth.*

THE END OF THE PATH

*LEFT: Borders of alliums and a laburnum
arch draw the eye toward a simple
stone plinth.*

STOP AND LOOK

*ABOVE RIGHT: Architectural spires of
Mahonia x media 'Charity' set against
a vivid rust-colored wall focus the eye
in a small garden.*

BEYOND THE ARCH

*RIGHT: A trellis arch frames a focal point
composed of an informal grouping of
raised beds, pots, and shrubs.*

Focal Points

Focal points within a garden invite you to explore further and entice you from one area of the garden to another. You don't have to use a man-made element to achieve this effect: an ornamental tree, or a group of shrubs or a stretch of water performs the same purpose, as will a combination of structure and plants – a plinth and urn filled with geraniums, for example, or an archway clad with roses framing an elegant bench beyond.

Distinctive plants within a border or flower bed can be used as a focus for the overall design, whether it's a spiky cordyline in a bed of frothy perennials or tall bronze fennel in a circle of low-growing herbs.

A focal point is a useful way of drawing the eye away from unsightly garden elements such as water tanks, compost heaps, or an ugly shed. Whereas a solid screen tends to draw attention to the fact that there is something behind it, an informal group of trees and shrubs centered on a garden seat shifts the focus to a more worthy subject.

Creating Height

Height is a vital ingredient for an interesting garden. Vertical features create space and movement by interrupting the view and concealing what lies ahead. Trees are a wonderful way of introducing height, but if you are planting from scratch, it will take a long time for a tree to grow to create the planned effect.

Man-made structures achieve instant effects: pergolas, arches, and summerhouses are all ways of raising the perspective. But don't overdo things: a collection of unrelated features makes a space muddled and incoherent, particularly in a small garden. Choose one or two simple features, and plant them with climbers that will disguise the framework and impose their own form and structure. An obelisk supporting a clematis and a rose that flower simultaneously draws the eye upward and introduces a nice color contrast.

On a smaller scale, you can bring a touch of drama to borders and flower beds by planting tall grasses, stately globe artichokes, and annual and perennial sunflowers, which grow well above head height.

REACHING FOR THE SKY

ABOVE: Trained sweet peas form a fragrant tower of pastel colors and supply the house with cut flowers for months.

TALL GRASSES

RIGHT: This striking border, dominated by colorful ornamental grasses, includes miscanthus, which can grow to 7 ft (2.1 m).

FULL HEIGHT

RIGHT: *The use of tall plants here prevents the high stone wall from upstaging the herbaceous border.*

Using Trees and Shrubs

Trees and shrubs are the natural structural elements of a garden, anchoring the planting in the landscape, and forming a basic framework that can then be filled out with herbaceous plants and annuals. Trees also provide valuable shade in summer; they give fruit, blossom, spectacular leaf color in fall; children love to climb them; and they support a whole microcosm of wildlife without which our gardens would be duller places.

When choosing a tree, think about its size, characteristic shape, and spread. Rounded trees such as the Indian bean tree make good specimen trees, planted singly in a lawn, as do weeping trees such as *Fagus sylvatica* 'Pendula'. The year-round appeal of evergreens is obvious but the leafless skeleton of a deciduous tree silhouetted against a wintry sunset should not be underrated. Providing color is an important part of the tree's role.

The sweet gum is renowned for its flaming leaves in fall while the yellow fruits of the crab apple *Malus* x *zumi* 'Golden Hornet' can persist on the tree well into the new year.

A TWIGGY CANOPY

OPPOSITE: *Dappled sunlight filters through the branches of a weeping birch, an ideal specimen tree for a lawn or beside water.*

SHRUBBERY FOR ACID SOILS

LEFT: *This complex tapestry of variegated and colorful shrubs and small trees is made up entirely of acid-loving plants.*

A PLANT FOR ALL SEASONS

ABOVE: Amelanchier lamarckii *makes an ideal tree or tall shrub for a small garden. It turns a glorious color in the fall, and is covered with blossom in spring and berries in summer.*

Beds and Borders

The best herbaceous beds and borders stand up to scrutiny all year round. For good results you'll need a framework of shrubs that includes a range of species – evergreens and berried shrubs for winter, early-blossoming bushes like Japanese quince, and some that herald fall with a fanfare of colored leaves. Add a succession of roses for scent and color all through summer, then turn your attention to underplanting. By growing a variety of spring bulbs, followed by herbaceous perennials and summer annuals, you can create a continuous display of flowers right up until the first frosts.

Bear in mind the orientation of your flower beds. Many shrubs can't tolerate early morning sun on frozen winter leaves; some of the taller herbaceous perennials, such as delphiniums and oriental poppies, grow weak and spindly in too shady a spot. Be sure to match plants to their soil requirements as well.

As long as you remember these few basic rules, your garden will have beautiful beds and borders that will provide enjoyment all year round.

A SPRING BORDER

LEFT: *Forget-me-nots and biennial wallflowers in restrained shades of yellow beneath a cloud of roses, combine to form a gentle color scheme that is easy on the eye.*

SUMMER FLOWERS

RIGHT: *Osteospermums are fast-spreading plants ideal for the front of a summer border. Remember that not all varieties are frost hardy.*

Winter

In winter you may have to look harder to appreciate your garden and train your eye to see beauty in an unconventional form. Skeletal shapes of trees, rose stems bristling with thorns, and wiry skeins of clematis set against a brooding sky all have a certain charm.

A light powdering of snow puts a whole new perspective on the garden, highlighting all the structural elements – walls, hedges, pergolas, obelisks – obliterating the planting, and revealing the garden's underlying framework more succinctly than any plans on paper.

Evergreens, particularly variegated species such as *Euonymus fortunei* 'Emerald 'n' Gold', provide welcome splashes of color against the unrelieved browns and gray of winter. The conical forms of spruce and pyramids of slow-growing yew keep their shape all year round. Hollies come into their own in winter and can be clipped as topiary or grown for cutting decorative greenery and berries for the house at Christmas. Dogwoods have

A TOUCH OF FROST

BELOW: *Leaves silvered with frost are a lovely sight on a cold winter's morning.*

Yew (*Taxus baccata*)

A WINTER BORDER

LEFT: *Colorful dogwood stems and* viburnum tinus *in bloom are set against a starkly sculptural backdrop of columnar conifers and an impeccably clipped yew hedge.*

A WOODLAND GARDEN
RIGHT: Hellebores are shade-loving plants and self-seed happily in woodland settings such as this. Flowers of Helleborus x hybridus *vary from white to every shade of pink and purple and are borne from mid-winter onward.*

A CARPET OF YELLOW AND WHITE
BELOW: Snowdrops and bright yellow winter aconites in their delicate green ruffs flower from late winter. For best results, plant them just after they have finished flowering.

Hellebore
(*Helleborus* x *hybridus*)

startlingly bright bare stems, while shrubs such as *Mahonia* x *media* 'Charity', wintersweet, *Garrya elliptica, Stachyurus praecox,* and *Viburnum tinus* all flower during the most unrewarding months of the year, and many of them are sweetly scented. Add the earliest flowering snowdrops, hellebores in muted shades of purple, pink and green, tiny inky-purple irises, and yellow winter aconites and you have a surprising number of flowers to welcome the start of another year.

Spring

Spring is the most exciting time in the gardening year. Trees and shrubs are hazy with the first green hint of leaves and the ground below is carpeted with flowers. Most of the flowering plants at this time of year are bulbs, which put on a brilliant show for a few weeks and then fade away back underground for another year.

Daffodils or narcissi are classic spring flowers, from the tiniest sprays of 'Baby Moon' and the curiously reflexed petals of *Narcissus cyclamineus* to the bold trumpets of 'King Alfred' that gladden the heart. Create a subtle color scheme with miniature daffodils, primroses, and white grape hyacinths; or make a bolder statement with deep purple tulips in a froth of white cow parsley.

SPRING SCHEME

ABOVE: A harmonious planting of yellow and delicate lemon narcissi with cool blue grape hyacinths.

BOLD AND BRIGHT

LEFT: Yellow wallflowers punctuated at random by pulsing red tulips create a stunning display.

BOWED DOWN WITH BLOSSOM

LEFT: *A mature specimen of an ornamental cherry,* Prunus 'Taihaku', *is an unforgettable sight at its flowering peak.*

A SPRING POSY

RIGHT: *A tiny group of spring flowers – pansies, apple blossom, and bluebells – is just enough to fill an egg cup.*

If you are prepared to delay mowing the grass until late in the season, crocuses, snowdrops, or snakeshead fritillaries can be planted in the lawn and left to naturalize to create an enchanting carpet of color.

Shrubs in bloom include spiky witch hazel, exquisite flowering cherries with classically simple flowers, or elaborate pompons of petals, and the electric yellow forsythia that shines like a beacon in suburban gardens everwhere.

MOSTLY WHITE

ABOVE: *A carefully orchestrated edging to a border of white tulips, alyssum, daisies, and hostas with variegated leaves.*

LATE DEVELOPERS

RIGHT: *Three plants of similar height but with very different flowers: sinister monkshood, simple open daisies, and yellow alstroemeria, all of which flower in late summer.*

SUMMER COMPANIONS

OPPOSITE: *Purple catmint and pink roses make perfect planting partners. Not only do their colors tone beautifully, but the sprawling catmint hides any unsightly bare rose stems.*

Ox-eye daisy
(*Leucanthemum vulgare*)

Summer

Herbaceous borders are the epitome of high summer, crammed with perennials, annuals and shrubs, and with the emphasis firmly on flowers. Old favorites such as roses, lilies, phlox, clematis, honeysuckle, and daisy-flowered helenium, all come up year after year and can be boosted by sowing annuals such as sweet rocket, marigolds, stocks, and clarkia.

A color scheme can help to keep a sense of order among all this profusion. A white border of roses, peonies, lilies, poppies, campanulas and silvery-leaved shrubs is inherently peaceful; while an extrovert grouping of red dahlias, penstemons, monarda, and roses will positively shout out its presence.

Scent is a strong feature in a summer garden, heady by day with the fragrance of roses and lilies, pinks, and sweet peas. In the evening, night-scented stocks, nicotiana, and jasmine will perfume the air, attracting both moths and appreciative humans.

The challenge in summer is to keep the borders blooming. Deadheading prompts plants to continue flowering, and cutting back spent delphinium stems will encourage a second flush of flowers. Keep pots of lilies or geraniums in reserve to plunge into gaps in borders, and rearrange sprawling plants to conceal dead or dying neighbors.

Late summer plants include monkshood, rudbeckia, Californian tree poppies, and bear's breeches, which will admirably compensate for plants that are past their best.

HERE COMES THE SUN
ABOVE: *Cheerful annual sunflower faces are a welcome sight in summer. They are easy to grow from seed and are ideal for children to plant.*

A RED SEA
LEFT: *A swathe of rusty red* Helenium *'Crimson Beauty' creates a patch of invaluable late summer color.*

OPPOSITE: *Dahlias, crocosmias, penstemons,* Salvia involucrata, *and Michaelmas daisies will keep a border in bloom from late summer to late fall.*

FIREWORKS IN THE SKY

LEFT: *Two trees for spectacular leaf color in fall:* Acer palmatum 'Ozakazuki' *and, in the background,* Liquidambar orientalis. *Acers are good all-round performers in a small garden – they are graceful, compact, and have extremely beautiful leaves.*

Fall

Color in the garden takes on a peculiar intensity at this time of year, especially at dusk. Red-hot pokers stand poised like rockets about to explode and the blazing leaves of Fothergilla major look fierce enough to scorch.

Michaelmas daisies flower in rich shades of crimson and purple, and spiky-headed dahlias flare away until cut down by the frost. Chinese lanterns are not fussy where they grow and their papery orange seedheads can be used to liven up dull corners. Balance these with shrubs such as cotoneaster or pyracantha, and you will not only get a good display of fall berries but you will also be providing birds and other small animals with vital winter food reserves.

Certain trees are the stars of the fall. The leaves of different varieties of *Acer palmatum* turn an unbelievable shade of scarlet, going out gloriously in a blaze of fireworks before winter's icy grip takes hold. Fallen ginkgo leaves are butter yellow and those of the sweet gum prismatic oranges and reds.

Dahlia 'Bishop of Llandaff'

Year-round Interest

If you plan your garden to include plants for every season, then it really should look good all year round. There are many ways of maintaining year-round interest. Bulbs, such as daffodils, can be relied upon to provide spring freshness, while perennials, such as oriental poppies, will give color year after year. Winter berries add flashes of red.

Use different leaves to provide a textural contrast by juxtaposing, for example, delicate fern fronds against rough giant gunnera leaves. Grow some trees for their bark alone – polished *Prunus serrula* and snakebark maple, for example.

Don't be in too much of a hurry to tidy up. Seedheads of fennel and poppies can be transformed by a silvering of frost on a winter's morning. The more practical benefits of leaving old flower stems in place include protecting next year's growth, and providing food for seed-eating birds. In some species the seedheads look better than the rather insignificant flowers, such as the papery thin disks of honesty and tall bristly teasels.

EVERGREEN SELECTION
ABOVE: Narrow-leaved rosemary and box complement broad-leaved mahonia.

Mahonia
(*Mahonia* sp.)

Daffodil
(*Narcissus* 'Soleil d'Or')

**WINTER
SEEDHEADS**
RIGHT: A selection of seedheads including ivy and honesty brings texture and interest during the winter months.

SEASONAL HIGHLIGHTS
RIGHT: Shrubs that change color in fall animate a woodland setting.

A PATCHWORK OF GREENS
BELOW LEFT: Conifers, heathers, and a smooth band of grass.

Yarrow
(*Achillea millefolium*)

Poppy seedheads
(*Papaver somniferum*)

Field poppy
(*Papaver rhoeas*)

Globe artichoke
(*Cynara scolymus*)

Teasel seedheads
(*Dipsacus fullonum*)

Skimmia
(*Skimmia japonica*)

DRY AND DUSTY

BELOW: The foot of a stone wall is one of the driest spots in a garden and perfect for succulent agave and South African osteospermums.

Sunny Sites

In general, sunny sites are the easiest to cultivate. Vast numbers of plants need to be grown in full sun to flower and fruit successfully. At most, they will need just a little extra attention when first planted – particularly watering – to help them get established. However, few sites are exposed to sun throughout the day: buildings, trees, and shrubs all cast a degree of shade, so bear this in mind when choosing your plants.

Some species have more precise requirements. Flag irises won't flower properly unless their rhizomes are baked by the sun; tough Mediterranean aromatic plants – rosemary, lavender, and thyme, plus shrubs such as cistus – like hot dry sites and poor, well-drained soil.

In a sunny garden that is exposed to extremes of weather, you will have to plant species that are drought resistant rather than simply sun lovers. Look out for plants that have silver leaves as these reflect the sun's rays and so avoid damage by scorching. Narrow-leaved plants, such as grasses and broom, are less

TOUGH CHARACTERS

LEFT: Alpine plants endure harsh conditions. This gravel bed is planted with Linum arboreum *and* Erinus alpinus.

SUN LOVERS

RIGHT: Free-draining gravel is an ideal medium for plants such as sun-loving thyme, flag irises, sisyrinchium, and sweet Williams.

prone to water loss by transpiration as their leaves have a small surface area in relation to their overall size. Species with large leaves soon wilt under the fatal combination of fierce sun and strong wind. Fleshy plants have evolved to conserve water, as have downy-leaved plants such as sages and lamb's ears. Alpine and seaside plants grow on very exposed sites in the wild and have inbuilt resistance to wind and sun.

A DESERT GARDEN

ABOVE: *Cacti are the outright winners when it comes to drought tolerance and are used to stunning sculptural effect in a Santa Barbara garden.*

GRAVEL GARDEN

LEFT: *A successful planting of species that tolerate arid conditions – agave, alliums, downy-leaved lamb's ears, succulent sedums, sage, genista, and ballota – is dominated by gray-leaved plants.*

Erigeron glaucus

This hot gravelly site is perfect for the sun-loving agave.

Houseleek (*Sempervivum* sp.)

Dry shade can be awkward. Trying to improve the soil by using manure and leafmold to boost its water-retaining properties is one way of tackling a dry shady site. The other is to work with the soil and grow the rather restricted range of species that will tolerate the conditions.

Ivy is a stalwart in such situations and can be supplemented with some ferns, plus delicate cyclamen for color in spring and fall. Shrubs can fill a dry shady border – try box, elaeagnus, and hypericum.

SHADE LOVER

ABOVE: Helleborus argutifolius *flowers from mid-winter until late spring in shady borders and also has attractive evergreen leaves with a slightly serrated edge.*

IN A WOODLAND GARDEN

LEFT: *Foxgloves like moist, humus-rich soil and will self-seed readily in the right conditions. Flowers from the Excelsior group come in a wide range of colors.*

325

Hosta fortunei var. 'Albopicta'

This shady haven includes aquilegias, lemon balm, and variegated geraniums.

Lungwort (*Pulmonaria rubra*)

Polypodium vulgare

Bluebells (*Hyacinthoides non-scripta*)

Plants for Shady Sites

Shade-tolerant plants can have fairly short flowering seasons, so foliage is important. Many shade species, such as hostas, have big leaves to catch the sunlight. Choose a variegated form for extra interest.

Different species of ferns grow in moist or dry shade and add texture and contrast. Variegated evergreen shrubs lighten dark corners – try *Euonymus fortunei* and *Elaeagnus*.

327

Garden
Themes

Flower Gardens

Flowers are the soft furnishings of the garden, bringing delightful color and texture wherever they are found. You can create endless themes based around flowers, ranging from the classic cottage garden to versatile cut flowers.

THE SOFT PALETTE
Roses, such as Rosa 'Peace' (above) *and the old rose* 'Fantin-Latour' (left), *are beautiful plants for the flower garden, adding a touch of color and magic.*

THE NEW ENGLAND LOOK

ABOVE: This marvellous rampant rose has been allowed to charge over the roof of a house. It is given added impact by the contrasting clumps of bright red, self-seeding poppies.

VERTICAL ACCENTS

LEFT: *Delphiniums are classic cottage garden plants bringing height and a variety of blues to the back of the border.*

Cottage Gardens

If you are aiming for a garden that is ebullient and informal – nature let loose but never allowed to take over, with climbing roses on the roof and foxgloves jumping out of the border – try the cottage garden. But be warned: it takes plenty of careful planning to recreate that random, carefree style.

The first trick is to create a garden full of secret places and surprises. Avoid having everything immediately visible the moment you step through the gate. Create gardens within gardens, avoiding the crisp and formal; send zigzag paths covered by arches and climbers all over the place so that visitors never quite know where they are going. The aim is for a garden that wraps itself around you: cottage gardens are gardens to get lost in.

Make sure that the planting is generous and let the plants spread without totally blocking their neighbors. Create distinctive spreads of color. The art is of skilled interference. The last trick is to buy plenty of scented plants. If possible, use the old varieties with powerful, lingering scents to perfume the air.

Stock
(*Matthiola incana*)

CLASSIC COTTAGE STYLE
LEFT: *The apricot-yellow Rosa 'Buff Beauty' has been very popular since it was introduced in the late 1930s. It is ideal for growing over an arch where you can catch its scent.*

Use annuals and biennials that self-seed readily. They pop up in unlikely places, creating new combinations of plantings and a delightful mix of color that keeps the garden looking lively. Fruit and vegetables, and berries and herbs, all add to the look, as do the many butterflies and bees attracted by the profuse flowers.

The ultimate hallmark is the reliance on old-fashioned materials, such as picket fencing, brick paths – use anything to extend the ambience of the garden.

ANNUALS IN THE BORDER

LEFT: *A bright, lively block of annuals and biennials – with pink and white foxgloves, red and blue cornflowers, purple campanulas, and sweet peas – sets the right balance between order and mayhem.*

A MAGICAL PATH

RIGHT: *Tall hollyhocks and pink lavatera give this path its own special atmosphere.*

THE PICTURE BOOK LOOK

BELOW: *The secret of success is excellent framing, here using pots and old roses.*

Larkspur (*Consolida ajacis*)

Clary sage (*Salvia viridis*)

Dog rose (*Rosa canina*)

A cottage border of hollyhocks in mixed colors with yellow verbascum.

Cottage Garden Plants

When choosing cottage garden plants you need shapes that are relaxed and informal, with plenty of tall, thin, gangly spires, and the ability to spread into clumps. The colors can be as loud or as soft as you like, either gently harmonizing or making marvellous sudden clashes. The plants illustrated here are traditional, failsafe ingredients.

Hollyhock (*Alcea rosea*)

Formal Flower Gardens

Walking around a formal flower garden, large or small, is just like inspecting the troops. The neat regular lines, uniform height, and predictability of a formal garden can be a very impressive sight, reflecting great control and an incredible attention to detail. The best way to create such a garden is by carefully mapping out the design. Include a certain amount of geometry and symmetry, and where the garden is overlooked by windows, make sure that it looks good from above. Use strong, structural plants to delineate the divisions using box or yew, for example, or even small smart conifers, and then infill with bright performers. For spring bedding nothing is better than tulips which come in a spectrum of colors from gorgeous soft lilacs to bright yellow. For a long summer of flowers use modern shrub roses that keep flowering until the frosts. Repeat plantings of the same variety give rhythm, authority, and substance. Avoid plants that self-seed, invade, climb, or spread wildly as the regular design should never be lost.

BOXED-IN ROSES

LEFT: *Box makes a great structural plant with its small, tightly packed leaves that can be clipped into all kinds of dense shapes. In this classic design they enclose pink hybrid tea roses. The gazebo completes the elegant picture.*

MINIATURE VERSAILLES

RIGHT: *With a few judicious details it is possible to create the Versailles look in a small city garden. The triangular arrangement of cubes leads the eye in to the focal point, a heather-topped classical urn.*

ARCHING GROWTH

ABOVE: *This white scented rose forms a beautiful, fragrant archway. It is neatly grown beside hybrid tea and shrub roses.*

THE GENTLE TOUCH

LEFT: *In this mix of soft colors and soft textures, pale pink roses are fronted by smooth, silky lamb's ears.*

BRIDGING THE GAP

RIGHT: *Here, roses have been planted in abundance to enhance a stream setting.*

The Rose Garden

Roses are quite possibly the best-loved of all flowers. There is an incredible range of roses in a bewildering array of colors and sizes. Before buying, check the flowering time, possible scent, dimensions and disease resistance. Inveterate spreaders such as creamy-white *Rosa filipes* 'Kiftsgate', can reach 50 ft (15 m) and may be used to provide a protective, floral hedge. Then there are old roses, which generally flower for a short period, with rich tangy scents. Ramblers, which send up long flexible stems from the base, are brilliant for growing through trees, and flower once each summer. The white 'Seagull' grows to 25 ft (7.5 m). Good climbers tend to be slightly shorter, about 15–20 ft (4.5–6 m), and are ideal for covering arches and pergolas because their stems can be trained into a network of branches.

There is an equally impressive choice if you have a small garden. Miniature roses, 18 in (45 cm) high, offer bright color. Then there are shrub, cluster, and large-flowered roses. But the star group are the English roses; they combine old-world looks and scent with the ability to flower gloriously all summer.

Rose
(*Rosa* 'Blessings')

Fragrant Gardens

The test of a really good garden is its range of delicious scents. At the tropical end you can have the smell of fresh pineapples from a Moroccan *Cytisus battandieri*, a vigorous, treelike shrub, reaching 15 ft (4.5 m), best grown against a warm, sunny wall where it gets covered by bright yellow flowers. For the smell of cloves you need dianthus; for burnt sugar and cakes try *Cercidiphyllum japonicum* which releases its smell when the leaves drop in the fall, and for an overwhelming perfume try philadelphus. You can have a scented garden right through the year from winter viburnums to spring daphnes, summer lilies, and the heliotropes that, if fed continuously, can keep on flowering into winter.

Dot highly perfumed plants around the garden so that you encounter different scents. There are some wonderful fragrances that are best enjoyed in seating areas: lilies, lilac, night-scented stock, lavender. Plant them in close proximity to benches or the windows of the house. When researching your choice of scented plants, make sure that you use the varieties with a traditional, strong fragrance. For example, when you plant sweet peas, use the highly-perfumed wild forms, rather than the less fragrant cultivars.

Lilac
(*Syringa vulgaris*)

NIGHT SCENTS

RIGHT: The joy of evening primrose is that you need plant only one; it will then seed itself around the garden, providing a glorious scent at night.

STRONG SCENTS

RIGHT: This curry plant, tumbling over the wall, releases a pungent perfume. Either side of the bench is strongly scented lavender.

This garden is enlivened by the sweet scent of the rose 'Crépuscule'.

Summer jasmine (*Jasminum officinale*)

Lily-of-the-valley (*Convallaria majalis*)

Sweet pea (*Lathyrus odoratus*)

Honeysuckle (*Lonicera periclymenum*)

Fragrant Flowers

Some flowers have such a good scent that they have never been improved upon. Lily-of-the-valley has been a major player in scented gardens since medieval times, as has the hardy garden jasmine since it reached the West in the mid-sixteenth century. Modern plant breeders have created stronger stems, larger flowers, and brighter colors, but they rarely come up with scents that rival these classics.

345

Flowers for Cutting

Try to save a part of the garden for growing flowers for cutting. If you are going to make plenty of displays through the year, group these flowers in separate beds, out of the way, where no one will spot the bare patches. Make sure that you provide easy access to the back of the bed to avoid trampling on the flowers.

The essential flowers you will need are daphne, forsythia, ivy, lilac, peony, tulip, and wisteria for spring; lady's mantle, lily, kniphofia, rose, salvia, and cardoon for summer; dahlia and sedum for the fall; and mahonia, viburnum, and Christmas rose for winter. The more you can grow the better.

The key to successful arrangements lies in how you treat your cuttings. Squash the stems so that they drink more water and keep them in a bucket of water until you are ready to begin. When making the composition start by selecting a theme, whether one-color, spare and elegant, or showy. That is best done by choosing your most eye-catching flower. Stand it

A SUMMER BASKET

ABOVE: *This posy uses roses – 'Gloire de Dijon' and 'Celeste' – with mahonia berries, senecio, and pelargoniums.*

HIGHLIGHT ON PASTELS

RIGHT: *This softly colored selection includes highly scented sweet peas, roses, scabious, and larkspur.*

GARDEN SCHEMES

OPPOSITE: *Tulips make ideal cut flowers for a spring display. Here, they are grown in a mixed border with forget-me-nots, pink bellis daisies, and plenty of wallflowers.*

slightly off-center, and work outward in all directions. With luck, when you have finished, all flowers will lead the eye back to the focal point. Try to avoid the temptation to pack in too many plants, forcing them into one tight container. Each flower should be kept separate, as far as possible, so that its form and color are visible. Make sure that all stems are below the water line, and regularly top up the water. To make the flowers stand up smartly use a special pre-soaked block, available from florists, into which the stems are easily inserted. Do not forget to include a selection of evergreens; they make exceptional 'linkers'.

SHINY LEAVES
RIGHT: The glossy leaves of choisya with Fatsia japonica *berries, pansies, and ranunculus.*

A SUMMER SPRAY
ABOVE: Lilies, columbines, roses, marigolds, and peonies.

Anemone (*Anemone pavonina*)

A SPRING SHOW
ABOVE: This fresh, home-grown arrangement features lilies, campion, delphiniums, and alliums.

TULIPS WITH RAFFIA
ABOVE: You do not need to be elaborate with flower arrangements. Red parrot tulips alone are quite stunning.

Delphinium
(*Delphinium* Belladonna
Group)

BUTTERCUPS
ABOVE: *Buttercups, picked from a wildflower garden, make a striking, bright display.*

FLORAL GARDEN ROOM
ABOVE: *A bright room like this, with plenty of ventilation, is ideal for keeping cut flowers to make floral arrangements.*

WIDE, WAXY PETALS
RIGHT: *For a bold, stylish arrangement concentrate on a few flowers such as this red lily, blue Dutch iris, and lisianthus.*

Water Gardens

Water gardens are magical. They give gardens an extra dimension, right down to the reflections on the pond surface in winter. No matter how small your garden, there is always room for some kind of water feature.

THE ULTIMATE SETTING
The marsh marigold (above) *is the first aquatic plant to flower in spring. It is essential for informal garden ponds* (left), *engulfed by large leaves and flowers.*

THE OCTAGON

ABOVE: This octagonal pool is bordered by profuse beds restrained by the paved path. Iris versicolor *grows in the water with a gorgeous spread of lilies.*

Formal Pools

Formal pools are a key part of the structure of your garden. If you want to see them at their very best, visit classic Renaissance-style gardens where water is used in two ways. Firstly, as a strong, static feature that doubles as a large-scale outdoor mirror to reflect the huge open sky and adjacent structures such as intricate, wrought iron gazebos. Their second role is as a high-profile spectacle of running water. This could mean jets spurting hundreds of feet in the air or long, stepped canals with water cascading down past statues rising up out of the water. You can use either, or both, of these two themes to create your own formal water garden.

There are three things to bear in mind to achieve the right look. Use brick or stone, formally laid in geometric patterns, for the edging and surroundings. Then think about the scale, so that the pool is correctly proportioned to the adjacent area. Finally, add a restrained choice of plants, together with a fountain or statue for a touch of grandeur.

SAN FRANCISCO SYMMETRY

ABOVE: *Everything is mirrored in this symmetrical garden. The water feature provides an elegant focal point for the whole area.*

THE SPANISH TOUCH

LEFT: *Small but stately fountains punctuate this tiled garden with a strong Moorish influence.*

WATER GARDENS

THE RAISED POOL

*RIGHT: The brick walls of
this formal, raised pool are
softened by evergreens, that
add year-round interest.*

ECHOING SHAPES

OPPOSITE: *This classic, long,
narrow pool reflects the
linear shape of the adjacent
hedge. The domed conifers
and tall flowers draw the
eye upward.*

White water lily
(*Nymphaea alba*)

A long, thin rectangular pool can be given extra style by standing architectural plants such as standard fuchsias or topiarized box at each corner, or by repeat planting right around the pool with potted patio roses, marguerite daisies, or petunias.

If you yearn for a formal pool design, but would like to create an effect that is slightly softer, the look can easily be mellowed by giving the eye some distractions. Plant up the cracks in the adjacent paving with the excellent, tiny, spreading, daisylike *Erigeron karvinskianus* with flowers that open white, turn pink and then purple, giving a carpet of three colors. Use grasses and bamboos to add height and interest with their leafy growth, or add potted brugmansias with their trumpet-shaped, scented flowers. To achieve a more unusual shape, create a pattern of pools with interlocking L-shapes or circular rills within rills. The pool remains the big attraction, but the overall effect is more subtle.

NATURAL SHAPES

RIGHT: *Irregular, natural shapes are ideal for informal pools. Here, the pool is surrounded by woodland plants to attract birds and insects. The pink and purple candelabra primula and dark-leaved ligularia provide bursts of color.*

CROSSING POINTS

OPPOSITE: *Across a wide pond you will need a bridge. It is not just for access, but makes a great vantage point where you can spot frogs, newts, and insects.*

Pickerel weed (*Pontederia cordata*)

Dwarf cat's tail (*Typha minima*)

GARDENER'S CHOICE

Pond Plants

A pond needs two kinds of water plant: the oxygenators to keep the water clear and control algae, and floaters, such as water lilies, that also combat algae. Make sure that they are not too vigorous for the size of your pond. Grow marginal plants for their flowers and to provide hiding places for wildlife.

361

WATER GARDENS

THE RAISED GARDEN

*RIGHT: A raised part of the garden
is given a novel twist with water
spouting into a small tank. The
umbrella plant provides the
framework for this simple design.*

MOSAIC POND

*ABOVE: This stylish mosaic pond is set
against a cobalt-blue wall inset with
mirror windows. The adjacent plants
provide bright reflections.*

Small Water Features

If you do not have the space for a large pond, there are plenty of small-scale alternatives, which also have the advantage of being safer if you have young children. Wall fountains look good and give the relaxing sound of falling water. You can buy them in kits with a classical look, such as a lion mask or the face of Neptune. Place an ornamental basin underneath, at the base of the wall, from where the water is pumped back up to the mouth again. For a really modern effect, try downward zigzagging, clear plastic pipes with dyed water swishing through, illuminated at night.

Millstone or pebble fountains are equally easy to make, and slightly more informal. They consist of a casual arrangement of large, smooth colored stones on the ground, set above a pump which pushes water up through them. The water drains down into a tank and is pumped back again. You can upgrade this idea using colored plastic balls, stained glass, or fragments of colored pottery, again with lighting at night. For an even more elaborate effect, a whole paved area could be encircled by pebble fountains.

ADAPTABLE URN

LEFT: The classical idea of a statue and plinth is given a watery slant using an elegant spray fountain.

Maze pools are also becoming increasingly popular. A 6 sq ft (0.5 sq m) area can be made into a shallow square pond containing an attractive chessboard arrangement of colored bricks. Frogs can hop in and out, it looks good from an upstairs window, filled with fractured reflections, and you can step over it without difficulty as you walk around the garden. Using long, thin rectangular pools like this is an excellent way of dividing up the garden.

However big or small your garden is, a water feature will enhance it, adding a valuable feeling of calm to your outdoor space.

Building a pebble fountain

Pebble fountains are quickly and easily made, and can be as wide as you want. The basic steps are set out below, but you can add extra ornamental touches besides those mentioned. The circumference can be highlighted using colored bricks or pebble arrangements set in concrete. You could even use pieces of mirror slightly set at upward angles to reflect the light in all directions, but guard against any dangerous edges.

1 *Begin by digging a hole slightly larger than required. Fill it with old carpet to protect against punctures, then add the preformed liner. Check the sides are level.*

2 *Place the pump in the center of the lined hole. It must be firmly wedged in place using bricks. Then connect the pump to the power supply.*

3 *Neatly arrange attractive colored shells, marbles, or smooth pebbles around the base of the fountain. Fill the liner with water, and switch on.*

SURPRISE FEATURE

LEFT: *An old millstone with pebbles surrounded by paving creates a fine feature in a kitchen garden. It is perfectly safe for children.*

BARREL PONDS

OPPOSITE: *Inexpensive and highly effective, this barrel is well planted with* Pontederia cordata, Geum rivale, *and variegated* Acorus gramineus.

THE WALL FOUNTAIN

RIGHT: *A ceramic fish trickles water onto a mound of beach pebbles.*

365

THE WHITE MARGINAL

ABOVE: The arum lily can stand in water up to 1 ft (30 cm) deep.

DAY LILIES

ABOVE: Hemerocallis 'Stella de Oro' grows in marshy conditions where it flowers prolifically from spring to the end of summer.

Planting Pond Edges

Half-hiding a pond behind tall plants that are subsequently mirrored in the water makes your pond into a surprise garden feature. The best plant for this trick is the *Dierama pulcherrimum*. The tiny round white corm you buy gives no hint of what is to come: a 4 ft (1.2 m) surge of arching stems with the most beautiful purple flowers.

Closer to the edge of the water you need water-loving plants. Their roots and bases stay under water, while the top growth is clearly visible. *Lysichiton americanus* thrives in muddy ground and flowers in early spring with a spike, half-hooded by a yellow spathe. If the soil is peaty and acid, try *Eriophorum angustifolium* which produces amazing summer flowers like white balls of 'cotton'. Purple-blue flag irises, rushes, and bulrushes are also part of the scene. Even *Canna glauca*, which has 16-in (40-cm) leaves topped by pale yellow flowers, can be grown in water in summer; but keep it dry over winter. Further away in the bog garden plant rheum, rodgersia, primulas, and *Miscanthus sinensis* 'Zebrinus' with its flash, white-banded foliage. Make the most of the edge of your pond – if carefully planted it can be one of the garden's greatest assets.

THE WILD LOOK

LEFT: *In the right conditions irises quickly multiply, forming wonderful, elegant clumps. Give them equally vigorous neighbors such as rodgersia.*

BRIDGING THE GAP

OPPOSITE: *This bridge, surrounded by marginal arum lilies, leads into another part of the garden.*

A gorgeous white iris and
lady's mantle provide
interest at the pond edge.

Yellow flag
(*Iris pseudacorus*)

Water Irises

If there is room for just one plant in or near water, make it the iris. They have distinctive, tall, thin shapes, and gorgeous flowers, often with the most intricate patterning. Choose from the *Laevigatae* group that includes blue *I. laevigatae*, yellow *I. pseudacorus*, purple-red Japanese *I. ensata*, and the American, purple-blue *I. versicolor*. Many beardless irises, such as the dark purple-blue *I. delavayi, also* look good when massed on a river bank.

Iris 'Sapphire Star'

Japanese water iris (*Iris ensata* Higo hybrids)

Blue flag (*Iris pseudacorus* x *versicolor*)

369

Dry Gardens

Dry sites can readily be turned into stylish, low-maintenance gardens. There are several different themes that can be easily incorporated into dry sites – desert gardens, alpine or rock gardens, pebble gardens, and gardens with minimalist style for providing cool and shady retreats.

THE WILD-WEST LOOK

These 'wild west' sculptural cacti at this Santa Barbara garden in California (left) look very impressive. The vicious prickly pear (above) has an intriguing form.

DRY GARDENS

FLOWERING YUCCAS

*RIGHT: Yuccas provide
startling accents. Plant
them in imposing groups
for best effect.*

GARDEN MAGIC

*BELOW: This wonderful array
of plants at Lotusland, in
southern California, is a
dramatic combination of
cacti and bromeliads.*

Desert Gardens

A desert garden will thrive where water is scarce. Scores of plants adore such conditions, star architectural plants that gardeners in cool areas with high rainfall long for. *Yucca whipplei*, from north-west Mexico, is one such plant. It makes dense rosettes of gray-blue spiked leaves, and when it flowers, powers up 10-ft (3-m) high stems packed with hundreds of lilylike flowers. Exhausted, it then promptly dies. The giant cactus, *Carnegiea gigantea*, is a columnar cactus that in the wild forms a massive pillar, 60 ft (18 m) high, but it grows so slowly that it is not a threat to the rest of the garden. Aeoniums are less dramatic. They can grow to 6 ft (1.8 m) with long, bare thin stems topped by incredible rosettes of leaves. For high style you need the dark purple-black *A. arboreum* 'Zwartkop'. It also makes a very good pot plant.

Succulents come in all shapes and sizes, and many send up 2-ft (60-cm) high long, thin flower stems hung with stunning tiny bright flowers: the echeverias are a brilliant example. There is nothing to beat a desert garden for bringing drama and a touch of style to a dry area.

AMAZING AGAVES

BELOW: In this sub-tropical garden, giant agaves thrive amongst the rocks and boulders in the glaring sunshine.

SUCCULENT CRAZY

LEFT: *Echeverias, with their olive-gray rosettes, are collectable items. They work in all kinds of garden, provided conditions are dry. You can even arrange them at the front of flower borders, forming a shapely hem.*

375

Alpines

Alpine plants make very good miniature gardens, a sort of lilliputian world where everything is scaled down, immaculate and neat. They are the intricate, small-scale side of gardening. The joy is in seeing such miniscule plants put out tiny exquisite flowers, and creating surprisingly bold effects.

Alpine gardens can be as small or as extensive as you like. Place them in tiny pots on the ground or display them in an alpine house on staging which makes handling infinitely easier. A good compromise is a well-drained raised bed, or a rockery. If you do not have well-drained soil, add a layer of gravel to speed drainage and help the soil to retain heat.

ALPINES WITH ATTITUDE
ABOVE: *A bright bold collection of armeria gives a lift to most displays.*

THE ALPINE SINK
RIGHT: Geranium cinereum *subsp.* subcaulescens *highlights this alpine display.*

Planting a rock garden

The best time to plant a rock, gravel, or scree garden is in late summer or even early fall. In those areas with cold wet winters – alpines particularly dislike the wet – wait until the weather starts to dry and the soil warms up in the spring. Waiting gives the young plants a far better chance of getting established, and of surviving these harsh conditions. Coming from high altitudes, they like the cold but need excellent drainage.

1 *Dig a hole slightly larger than the plant's rootball. Loosen the soil at the hole's base to help the roots spread, and to facilitate drainage. The soil should be light and sandy.*

2 *Sit the plant in the hole, having watered the soil if it is dry. The top of the soil must be level with the ground around it. Fill in, firm down, water, and sprinkle gravel around the stem.*

Lithodora diffusa 'Cambridge Blue'

Spanish dagger (*Yucca gloriosa*)

Eryngium giganteum

Sempervivums in the dry garden.

Plants for Dry Sites

There is a surprisingly wide range of plants for dry sites, including many Mediterranean species. Specialist books list hundreds of 'dry' candidates, and most are readily obtainable. Topping the lists are the alliums, many crocuses, eryngiums, euphorbias, hebes, irises, salvias, and herbs such as bay and thyme. Garlic is also easily grown. Just break off the bulbs, plant them out over winter, and by next summer they will be juicy, fat, and ripe.

Saxifrage (*Saxifraga* x *apiculata*)

Cool and Dry

A cool, dry garden projects an enviable sense of calm and tranquility. The ultimate cool look has its roots in Islamic gardens, where protective, high walls with a giant door enclose an amazingly elaborate, hugely artistic creation with ornamental tiles – no grass in sight, arched cloisters, a canal or fountain of water, and fruit trees. Most gardens used the same model, but with added variations. You can apply some of these ingredients to your garden to create a retreat from the fierce heat of the sun and seek cool comfort in the shade of an elegant palm tree.

Use patterned, frost-proof tiles on walls, erect arched pergolas, and create spare inner gardens using one or two key props, such as potted plants with cool foliage. Water features give the sensation of cool calm, and you can produce a wonderful effect using a pool enircled by palms or a gentle, wall-mounted fountain. Some of these features can be adapted for a more modern look, reflecting minimalist architectural styles and using sculptural plants to add areas of interest and shade.

RIGHT ANGLE DESIGNS

LEFT: *The minimalist style of this Los Angeles garden echoes the surrounding architecture to provide a cool retreat.*

FLOWING DESIGNS

ABOVE: *This Spanish-style inner courtyard provides shade, shape, patterns, clever planting, and, above all, complete privacy.*

THE JAPANESE WAY

ABOVE: This gravel garden incorporates Japanese elements, with a fluid swirl of moss.

SPARE AND BEAUTIFUL

RIGHT: An artist's garden on Long Island revels in the uncluttered. An expanse of gravel ties the different features together.

LEFT: *Dry gardens need not be devoid of foliage or water. Here, carefully placed yew adds a cooling touch of green, while the pond features arum lilies and irises.*

MOSAICS

BELOW: *This home-made mosaic birdbath adds fun and color to the dry gravel garden, and is reflected in the tiles that follow the path and edge the garden.*

Gravel Gardens

Gravel or stone gardens require minimal maintenance, and can make unusual and exciting features. Out of this flat, smooth swirl pop up rocks and boulders and island beds to wander round. Complementary plants include Mediterranean thin, vertical conifers, rosemary, poppies, giant grasses such as *Stipa gigantea* growing 6 ft (1.8 m) high, and the ankle-high *Hordeum jubatum*, with silky white plumes and a purple tinge at the end. Because everything stands out as highly engineered, you can add all kinds of *objets d'art* such as circles of vertical colored poles, mirrors hanging from branches, and stained glass catching the sun. Gravel gardens thrive on being theatrical. The gravel brings out the best in whatever stands on it.

Oriental Style

Japanese gardens are not just stylized gardens, they are spiritually coded places, and scaled-down copies of Japanese landscapes. If you wish to recreate an authentic oriental garden, balancing the *yo* and the *in*, the *yin* and the *yang*, you will need to refer to specialist books. If, however, you would like to incorporate oriental style and simplicity into your existing garden, there are a few features that will bring it all together.

Views are the key ingredient. Plant as many shrubs and trees as you like in the garden, but do not allow them to grow into solid, impenetrable blocks as you have to be able to see through them. To create a view, build a mini hill, approximately 6 ft (1.2 m) high, from banked-up soil at the edge of the garden. Place a small bamboo hut at the top giving views across the garden.

Pruning is an important task in an oriental garden. Either take out branches to leave a tracery, or try Japanese

CREATING THE ESSENCE
LEFT: *The elegant, open-branched tree, bamboos, low-level compact planting, statuary, and an ornamental path are the hallmarks of a classical Japanese garden.*

FLASH OF COLOR
ABOVE: *All oriental gardens need bridges. They can be tiny, dwarf structures over the thinnest canals. Paint them as bright as you like.*

385

BARE BAMBOOS

RIGHT: The see-through view at its best, using giant bamboo canes.

STILL WATERS

LEFT: The elegant corner of this Japanese garden includes bamboo fencing and stepping stones, azaleas, conifers, and ferns.

cloud pruning. This means stripping all the foliage off a few bare stems and leaving a ball of foliage at the top, bobbing about in the sky. There is no fixed list of oriental plants. Japanese cherries and bamboos are ideal, but other plants are just as suitable, such as Lawson's cypress, reduced to six bare stems topped by a cluster of leaves.

The final ingredients are oriental statuary with tiny stone bridges and lanterns, and ornamental, stylized paths. Each stretch should be slightly different, using stones in varying patterned arrangements.

POTTED STYLE

ABOVE: Small, container gardens can include oriental style. Here, the bamboo Fargesia murieliae 'Simba' is grown in a dragon-patterned pot.

THE ZEN GARDEN

RIGHT: The main feature is well-raked sand, pebbles, and the judicious use of rocks. Here, the surface is neatly framed by large stones and lengths of hollow bamboo.

Woodland and Wild Gardens

It is not essential to have a huge space to create your own woodland or wildflower garden. Even small areas have one or two suitable pockets of damp shade, or spare banks that are ideal for growing an abundance of colorful flowers.

THE NATURAL THEME
Wildflower meadows (left) *provide the perfect opportunity for going back to nature. Plants such as field poppies* (above), *attract all kinds of wildlife.*

Protect lots of things with GEICO.

Thousands of people are unknowingly paying more than they should for insurance. Are you one of them?

You know GEICO insures cars, but you could also save big when we insure your **motorcycle, ATV, RV** or even **commercial** vehicle. Plus, we can help you with **boat, personal watercraft insurance and more** through the GEICO Insurance Agency.

Go to **geico.com**, call **1-800-841-3000** or contact your **local GEICO agent** for a FREE rate quote. In just a few minutes, you'll find out how much you could save with GEICO. Why spend anymore than you have to?

WITH GEICO, IT'S EASY TO SAVE.

Sure, extra money in your pocket is valuable, but so is your time. And we get that. That's why it only takes 15 minutes to find out how much money you could save with GEICO. Go to **geico.com.** Answer some quick questions and get an accurate rate quote. Then start your policy **online, over the phone, or at a local office** — whatever you're most comfortable with.

IT'S NOT JUST SAVINGS. IT'S SAVINGS AND SERVICE.

You could save hundreds with GEICO – but did you know that GEICO has friendly service online or over the phone depending on how you like to do business? If you prefer a local touch, you can contact your local GEICO agent. You can also file and track your claim online.

DEPENDABILITY. IT'S WHAT WE'RE MADE OF.

Some people see GEICO as a "new" insurance company. The thing is, we've been consistently protecting drivers and delivering great value for 75 years. So you can count on us for the long term.

Visit **geico.com**, call **1-800-841-3000** or contact your **local GEICO agent** now for a FREE rate quote.

See how much money you could save!

Under the Trees

A cool, shaded woodland, with a carpet of bulbs and shade-loving perennials, will turn your garden into a haven for both you and the local wildlife to enjoy. Plenty of plants will thrive in cool, damp shade, especially if the light is dappled. You can create a miniature woodland, with bright sparks of flowers beneath the trees. Dense, dry shade can be more difficult to enliven; try arums, ivies, and periwinkles, adding plenty of organic compost or leafmold on the ground as a thick mulch to keep in whatever moisture is present.

When choosing which trees to grow, you can go with native varieties, but since most gardens use imported plants somewhere, you might as well grow ornamental cherries, acers, and eucalyptus. The more open the branches the better for letting in shafts of light, and giving the plants a chance. Darker, shady areas under thick spreading trees can add a good touch of the Gothic, but without any intervention you may end up with vicious, head-high piles of brambles.

SPRING WOODLANDS
BELOW: The wild primrose always gives a good show, adding color in the shade.

SHADY SHRUBBERY
LEFT: Both rhododendrons and azaleas guarantee high-profile, bright spring color. They thrive in the cool shelter of woodlands where the soil is acid.

THE WOODLAND GARDEN
OPPOSITE: Mind-your-own-business and ferns edge this woodland path, where dappled sunlight filters through the trees.

391

Wildflower Meadows

You can recapture the natural beauty of a wildflower meadow in your own garden, with scatterings of colors and grasses, light and dark greens, greens verging on blue, punctuated with rainbow-bright flowers.

The more seed of endangered native species you sow the better, but beware of using too many quick-growing annuals that will not provide a long-term planting, or relying on robust plants that may dominate. You need an extremely good mix. To replicate an established spring and/or summer flowering meadow, buy seed from a nature reserve or specialist catalog. Get the right seed for your soil and climate. Start by tackling perennial weeds, remove the turf and topsoil to reduce the fertility, break up the surface and rake it.

DAISIES

LEFT: *A mass of daisies recreates the prairie with its sea of yellow and white blooms.*

SELF-SEEDING POPPIES

ABOVE: *Here, poppies have been allowed to self-seed naturally, forming a multi-colored carpet.*

THE MINI MEADOW

ABOVE: This is the perfect example of how a large-scale effect with drifts of poppies, white daisies, heartsease, and cornflowers, can be packed into the smaller garden.

Sow the seed in fall. For the first, invariably flower-free year keep the growth height to about 3 in (8 cm), and the following years only mow when the flowers have set seed. Cut back summer meadows in the fall.

Some wildflower meadows are very hard to get going, but once they take off they virtually look after themselves. The great blocks of bright flowers and random scatterings are something you never get in a regular garden, certainly not on such a staggering scale.

Ox-eye daisy
(*Leucanthemum vulgare*)

THE WILD LOOK

ABOVE: *This is a perfect combination for the wildflower garden: wild sweeps of single colors and shapes. From front to back: cow parsley, poppies, and grasses.*

THE DAMP MEADOW

LEFT: *There are wild flowers for most conditions. This moist stretch of land contains candelabra primulas, hostas, irises, and polemonium.*

HIGHS AND LOWS

ABOVE: *Ragged robin, daisies, and buttercups, backed by the tall thin spires of verbascum, create a wildflower area alongside the garden path.*

MEADOW SEAT

LEFT: *An exuberant show of buttercups, white campion, and foxgloves at the wild end of the garden.*

THE WILD TRAIL

RIGHT: *An informal path winds through blocks of ox-eye daisy, musk mallow, and chamomile.*

Wildflowers in the Garden

Wildflowers have a beauty and charm that is unrivalled in the garden. There is a myth that wildflowers demand big spaces, but any spare patch of the garden will do, even one at the end of a border. Make the nature garden a strong contrast between the well-planned and organized beds and borders, where every flower is carefully tended, and the unrestrained informality of the wilderness. You will need a buffer zone between the two where the planting gradually becomes much more fluid, such as an area of lawn.

Daisies, evening primrose, foxgloves, harebells, ragged robin, spurge, and phlox are all terrific plants, attracting plenty of wildlife, but you also need to inject some grasses: the dwarf, the tall, the wispy, the flowering, the floppy and vertical. Grasses can be dual purpose: don't cut them back in the fall, but leave some stems sticking up over the winter – they will keep interest alive, casting shadows, and sparkling in the frost.

Maintaining a wildflower site

Once a year scythe down the growth, after the flowers have seeded. If the site develops any large bare patches, carefully fork over the soil and plant perennials or sow a few annuals. Poppies make an exceptional show. Cover the ground with chicken wire to keep the birds away, and water well.

1 *Cut the long grass and flower stems in late summer if you want the flowers to set seed, or earlier if not, followed by regular mowings until late fall.*

2 *After you have scythed down the long grass, leave it where it falls on the ground to be dried by the sun. It can be raked and removed once dried.*

Cowslip (*Primula veris*)

Corn poppy (*Papaver rhoeas*)

Shasta daisy (*Leucanthemum* x *superbum*)

Wildflowers

Research your choice of wildflowers carefully. Planting native species will make a positive contribution to the environment. There are wildflowers for dry and damp sites, for chalk and acid soil, and for shade and bright sun. Armed with these facts you stand every chance of success. Make sure that you choose plants that will flower right through the growing season.

A butterfly garden with daisies, fritillaries, and cowslips.

Cornflower (*Centaurea cyanus*)

Wildlife Gardens

Many gardens, whether woodland or wild, formal or informal, will invariably attract a certain amount of wildlife. You can further encourage beneficial insects and bees, beautiful butterflies, birds, and animals by providing them with a few of their favorite plants.

The first step is to ensure that you are providing the right conditions to entice the wildlife, and that once it arrives it will stay. Water features are a magnet for all sorts of creatures, from frogs and toads to dragonflies and beetles. Ponds need one gently sloping side – frogs can hop into a sheer-sided pond but they will not be able to hop out. They also need nearby 'apartments' of scattered bricks and stones with damp, shady hideaways where they can escape the sun, and find a meal of slugs. Always include oxygenating plants, such as water starwort or Canadian waterweed, in your pond. They keep the water healthy by discouraging algae and also provide shelter and shade for pond life.

BENEFICIAL BEE

ABOVE: Attracting bees into your garden will benefit all the plants.

POND LIFE

RIGHT: Water lily leaves make ideal landing pads for wildlife such as frogs and toads.

A NATURE RESERVE

LEFT: Here, unchecked wildflowers and grasses surround a pond packed with fish and amphibians.

To observe the wildlife in your garden without making your presence too obvious, it may be worth building a hide or a camouflaged place to watch from. Badgers, straight out of their holes, are extremely timid and alert. Watch with sensitivity.

On a smaller scale, it is often delightful to sit and birdwatch. To encourage birds into your garden, provide them with a sheltered place to eat and a bath to drink and bathe in. Position a nesting box or bird table in a safe place, and bear in mind the agility of any neighborhood cats. Birds will have a feast in a garden with plenty of seedheads in the fall.

Leave fallen logs, snapped-off branches, holes in stone walls, anywhere creatures can hide. Each place has its own inhabitants and builds up the food chain with worms and beetles, slow-worms, mice and voles, rabbits, foxes, and sparrowhawks. With time and patience the wildlife garden becomes a place of buzzing, humming sounds, of calls and shrieks, and strange croakings late at night. It generates its own special magic.

Putting up a nesting box

Nesting boxes for birds and bats are readily available in a variety of sizes, but if you want to attract one particular species, make your own so that it meets its needs. The floor should be at least 16 sq in (100 sq cm). Nail it high up on a mature tree in the spring. It might take up to three years to colonize.

1 *Always begin by checking that the dimensions of the nesting box, in particular the width, are not too wide for the tree. A secure box offers better protection than a nest.*

2 *You need a 2-in (5-cm) nail to fix the box to the trunk which should be over 8 in (20 cm) diameter Do not use young trees because they can be easily damaged.*

THE SECLUDED NESTING BOX

LEFT: *The ideal site for a nesting box gives the inhabitants seclusion and privacy, and a ready supply of food with plenty of seedheads and insects nearby.*

BIRDBATHS

RIGHT: *Ornamental birdbaths are eye-catching focal points as well as providing somewhere for the birds to drink – vital in long, dry summers.*

Attracting Butterflies, Bees, and Birds

Butterflies like lapping up nectar with their long, uncoiling tongues. Besides well-known magnets such as buddleias and sedum, provide a range of flowers such as Joe-pye weed, milkweed which is an excellent source in midsummer, and yarrow. Bees enjoy the same plants, as well as eryngium, oregano, thyme, and wild clover, and as many fruit trees as you can muster. But note that a beehive in the garden does not instantly guarantee continuous buzzing, as bees may fly up to three miles away to collect nectar.

Birds need protective nesting sites with high dense growth such as forsythia or a mixed hedge, which attracts all kinds of wildlife, made from beech, corylus, dogwood, and oak where they are safe from cats and predatory birds. They also need a good range of berrying plants to feed on. Blackthorn, common holly, black elder, common ivy, and the spindle tree all offer an excellent diet.

Sage (*Salvia*)

Butterfly bush (*Buddleja alternifolia*)

THE NEW YORK ASTER

RIGHT: *The pinkish-red* Aster novi-belgii *provides a good source of nectar for butterflies, like this tortoiseshell, from late summer to mid-fall.*

Phacelia tanacetifolia

Home Produce

Growing your own produce gives you the choice of selecting your favorite varieties of fruit, vegetables, and herbs to supply your kitchen. A vegetable garden is always rewarding and even the smallest space can yield crops from containers. You can also make sure your food is organically grown.

LOOKS GOOD, TASTES GOOD
Vegetable gardens can be bright and attractive (left) *with pumpkins, nasturtiums, and sunflowers. Shiny ripe tomatoes* (above) *add a splash of red.*

HARVEST TIME

ABOVE: *This productive kitchen garden has potatoes and onions, with decorative beans shooting up tall canes.*

Kitchen Gardens

Kitchen gardens can be incredibly productive if you plan them carefully. Think about the layout and your type of soil, adding fertilizers where necessary. Rotate your crops so that nothing is grown on the same spot for more than two years. This prevents the build-up of certain pests and diseases whose life cycles can be easily disrupted by growing unrelated crops; it also avoids the depletion of particular nutrients.

The most surprising thing about kitchen gardens is that there are so many crops to grow – you nearly always need twice as much space as you thought. When planning your crops, start with several seed catalogs, and see what is on offer. Asparagus, green and purple broccoli, tender carrots, red-patterned Italian radicchio, frizzy-leaved endive, lettuces with names like 'Rossa di Trento' and 'Little Leprechaun', mangetout, bush tomatoes with tiny yellow fruit – the list goes on and on. You also need to allow for space between each plant to let it fatten, and to facilitate weeding.

GEOMETRIC BEDS

ABOVE: This well designed, small-scale kitchen garden is edged by clipped box.

VEGETABLES WITH COLOR

RIGHT: If you have an adjacent plot of ground why not grow creeping nasturtiums to add bright red flashes, and marigolds to add yellow? They also help to keep down the weeds.

413

PEPPERMINT

ABOVE: Herbs are essential in the kitchen garden; use them to fill any spare gaps. Mint should be planted in sunken buckets as it spreads rapidly.

Broad bean (*Vicia faba*)

MIXED PLANTINGS

RIGHT: Even in a small space, you can grow decorative vegetables interspersed with flowers.

APPLE ORCHARD

ABOVE: It is always tempting to grow several apple trees with different varieties, but one tree alone will produce hundreds of apples. Far better to choose a special multi-variety tree with two or three kinds grafted on.

Fruit is best included around the boundary of the kitchen garden. Apples can be grown as 'step-overs', which means they are bought ready-trained as knee-high vertical stems with branches shooting off to the sides at right angles. They make a miniature fence. Blackberries can be grown as fans along wire fencing, gooseberries as a single short vertical stem underneath a tall 'U' shape, and pears as cordons growing at an upward angle of 45 degrees. The secret of success is knowing how to pack everything in.

414

Herb Gardens

The taste and scent of herbs is essential in any kitchen. Herbs also make decorative garden plants in their own right and a herb garden can be an attractive addition to your planting scheme. Herb gardens are traditionally designed using plants contained in ornamental compartments, divided by herringbone paths and clipped box, and laid out inside triangles, circles, and oblongs. They are much easier to pick if you provide easy access.

Dedicated herb growers can group together herbs for particular purposes: culinary varieties for the kitchen, a selection for aromatherapy (tie together the stems of lavender, rosemary, and mint, and hang them under the hot tap for a relaxing bath), for potpourri (using sage, thyme, chamomile), and mild natural medicines (always check with your doctor first).

When drying herbs for out-of-season use, pick them early in the morning, on a warm day, when the dew has

HERBAL SPLENDOR
LEFT: *This impressive herb garden contains large clumps of purple sage, fennel, chives, and catmint.*

SCENT AND COLOR
ABOVE: *Here, the round, edible leaves of nasturtium contrast with the spiky foliage of rosemary.*

417

THE WELL-STOCKED KITCHEN

*ABOVE: Herbs for the kitchen come in several guises: fresh
from the garden, flavoring olive oils and vinegars, and dried.*

Basil
(*Ocimum basilicum*)

FORMAL DESIGNS

LEFT: *This traditional herb garden design has an oval scheme intersected by attractive brick paths, and a focal point in the center. The herbs radiate outward.*

COLORFUL GROUPINGS

BELOW: *Rosemary combined with creeping thyme, purple sage, lavender, and pink pelargoniums make an attractive herb bed.*

just dried, with the flowers on the verge of opening. Handle them gently, without bruising. The quickest drying method is using a microwave, which takes from 1–3 minutes depending on the leaf sizes. Watch them carefully. Oven drying takes approximately 2 ½ hours at 55°F (13°C). Alternatively, hang bunches of herbs in a dry, well-ventilated room for several days.

When storing dried herbs use clean, cool, dry glass jars. Check that there is no condensation (if so, re-dry), and only keep for about twelve months. Since the drying gives a concentrated strong flavor, add with care to recipes.

Rosemary (*Rosmarinus officinalis*)

Chives (*Allium schoenoprasum*)

A pastel color grouping of poppies, borage, and dill.

Variegated marjoram (*Origanum vulgare* 'Gold Tip')

Curled parsley
(*Petroselinum crispum*)

GARDENER'S CHOICE

Culinary Herbs

Culinary herbs are easy to grow, taking up minimum space. They really add that extra fresh flavor to a meal, and with repeat sowings over the summer guarantee a continuous supply. It is now possible to grow all kinds of specialist herbs, but a group of basil, chives, mint, oregano, parsley, rosemary, sage, and thyme is usually more than adequate.

THE MEDITERRANEAN CORNER

BELOW: *A young, standard rosemary dominates this herb group of cotton lavender and parsley. The scene is embellished by large, smooth round stones.*

THE GREAT BAY

RIGHT: *Bays can be easily trained to reach this impressive shape in a large pot. Either let them reach the right height and then prune, or gradually style them as they grow, without stripping off too many leaves which provide the plant with energy.*

Container Ideas

No available space in the garden? Do not worry. You can easily grow scores of herbs and vegetables in pots. In fact, some look far better individually highlighted, especially rosemary which can be very architectural. If left alone it may grow out of control, but with careful trimming you can create a smart, open shape. Bay also looks good growing in pots, particularly when it has been topiarized into a smooth mushroom or an elegant mophead.

Since large pots can be expensive, why not grow salad crops in buckets with added drainage holes? If you want an early supply, but don't have cloches, grow salad crops in buckets indoors in early spring for planting out the moment the frosts have passed. Cordon tomatoes can be grown in pots as a vertical stem, or trained in an upward zigzag. Nip out the growing tip to send up a shoot 45 degrees to the right, then nip out another to send it back again, and so on. Tie it to wires on a wall. Bush or trailing tomatoes are less fiddly, and are also ideal for containers, as are baby carrots, dwarf gooseberries, peppers, radishes, salad rocket, spring onions, and strawberries. Lack of space does not mean missing out on flavor.

DECORATIVE DISPLAYS

ABOVE: *This ornamental shallow pot is ideal for a selection of kitchen herbs on a window sill.*

EYE-CATCHING TOMATOES

LEFT: *A pot of bright red cherry tomatoes raised on a plinth makes a feature in a small garden.*

423

PATTERNS WITH LETTUCES

ABOVE: *The increasing range of red lettuces means that it is now quite easy to create decorative effects in the kitchen garden.*

A CLASSIC POTAGER

RIGHT: *This unusual potager uses long, wide uncluttered paths, attractive bricks, and well-spaced plants in the beds, mixed with garden flowers.*

Ornamental Potager

The ornamental potager is an attractive mix of vegetables and flowers growing together, and has a long distinguished history going back to the mid-sixteenth century. Villandry, the great French Renaissance chateau, is an example of a grand-scale potager with nine huge square beds, each edged by box, containing flamboyant schemes within.

The key tactic when planning a potager is to rely heavily on annual flowers, which means you can be flexible with each year's design. Do not feel hemmed in by tradition by relying on clipped box to provide the structure; use great clumps of parsley instead or rows of pink-flowered chives, or heliotrope to fill the air with scent. Perennial herbs can also be used as sectional divisions. And use plants for height, such as clematis climbing up frames, and the tall feathery fennel, while making use of different leaf colors, such as those of red lettuces, to add pattern. Peas and beans growing up wigwam frames can be supplemented by French marigolds at their base to add a highlight of color.

Chives
(*Allium schoenoprasum*)

EMPHASIS ON COLOR

LEFT: *A clever mingling of chives and alliums interspersed with marigolds gives the potager color. The beans are trained up an obelisk, and the apples grown imaginatively over an arch.*

425

Aubergine
(*Solanum melongena*)

Growing Vegetables

Vegetables are as good as the soil they grow in. If you can, create raised beds framed by specially treated timber that looks good and helps hold back all the extra well-rotted manure and compost which gets thrown on top each year to improve the soil structure and fertility. One of the best natural composts-cum-soil conditioners you can add is leafmold. Collected in great piles and contained in wire bins, the leaves gradually rot down, to form a potent, crumbly mix.

Thin, free-draining sandy soils quickly lose moisture and nutrients so they need bulking up. Thick, solid clay also needs help to open up the soil; adding mushroom compost speeds up the process. What you must not do, having created a rich, organic mix for the vegetables with plenty of oxygen and wormlife, is to walk all over it. The soil structure will be compacted and ruined. Make sure that the beds are not so wide that you cannot reach the center comfortably. A new bed will need digging up and weeding, with manure dug in, but thereafter that should not be necessary. Compost scattered on the surface will get dragged down by the worms. All the hard work is done.

Carrots
(*Daucus carota*)

Sowing seeds

Begin by marking out the line of each drill using string tied to two pegs, or a length of wood placed over the ground. Next, rake out all the large stones, working the soil down to a fine tilth. As a general guide, drills for a 24–30 in (60–75 cm) wide crop should be 24 in (60 cm) apart, and 8 in (20 cm) wide. Sow the seeds at the recommended distances, or closer for subsequent thinning, cover with soil, and keep watered.

1 *Take your time when raking. Large stones need to be removed, and clods of soil broken up. Next, use a hoe to make a smooth, flat bed for the seeds.*

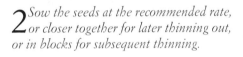

2 *Sow the seeds at the recommended rate, or closer together for later thinning out, or in blocks for subsequent thinning.*

3 *Thin out seedlings as soon as necessary or the adjacent plants will suffer. They do not just need space to grow, but must be given all the available light.*

REGULAR CROPS

LEFT: *Here, quick-growing, tasty lettuce seedlings have been planted in a spare bed to provide instant replacements for a crop that has been picked.*

427

HOME PRODUCE

EASILY ACCESSIBLE

RIGHT: This sequence of small beds is perfect for quick picking and makes an attractive kitchen garden.

Salad Crops

Lettuces are the main salad crop, and they come in two basic kinds. The non-hearting 'come-and-cut-again' type, when you simply take as many leaves as you require, leaving the plant to grow on in the ground, and the dense, hearting group which includes crisp icebergs, butterheads, and cos. If you have sufficient space, grow a couple of each kind. Sow seed every fortnight, to give a constant summer supply. If you over-sow, use the thinnings in a salad. It is important that you water during any long dry spells as most lettuces quickly bolt, becoming strangely misshapen with a bitter taste.

Endive (which is frilly-edged) for summer or winter eating, chicory, and radicchio (red chicory) for fall–winter consumption, are all good-looking salad crops. Red-stemmed chard is extremely colorful with flash red stems and veining, and shiny dark green leaves which make an impressive show in any dish. It is very useful in winter, in stews and Italian cuisine. Greenhouse tomatoes also have a long life, hanging on through the fall.

Tomato
(*Lycopersicon esculentum*)

Cucumber
(*Cucumis sativus*)

429

Fruit

The best fruit gardens are enclosed by high, south-facing walls against which the pears and plums, apricots and figs can be grown. The extra heat helps the fruit ripen more quickly. In fact, brickwork is not essential, but shelter certainly helps. Avoid shady sites and areas prone to late frosts.

Some fruit trees have special needs. Figs can send down long, vertical, thick tap roots that help to propel the cultivar into a giant tree. To prevent it taking off, make sure that it is well contained in a stone-lined pit or a large barrel. Fig varieties range from the tender to the relatively hardy, with the juicy fruit white or black.

Pears will fruit any time from summer to early winter, depending on the variety chosen, while plums and gages generally finish in the early fall. Cherries are too rarely grown; 'Morello' is the most popular variety, and the best culinary cherry for making cherry brandy and jams. If you haven't room for a fruit tree, try to find a spot for some strawberry plants. They are highly productive for two years, before collapsing exhausted. Keep renewing your stock. Raspberries and other soft fruits can also be grown.

THE TASTY TRIO
ABOVE: These types of strawberry, 'Elsanta' (top), 'Elvita' (below), and the tiny sweet alpine (right), can be grown in cracks between paving.

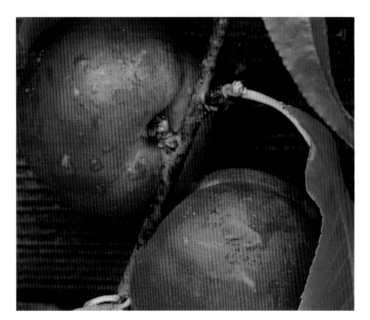

'MORELLO'
OPPOSITE: Cherry trees are highly productive, giving 12–20 lb (5.4–9 kg) from a fan-trained tree, and double that from a bush.

NECTARINES
LEFT: Nectarines have smoother skins than peaches. In cool climates they must be grown in a gently heated greenhouse.

The Garden Calendar

Regular maintenance in your garden will keep it looking neat and tidy and your plants will stay healthy and strong. Use this calendar as a quick guide to keeping your garden in good condition throughout the year. Before selecting plants, assess your soil type and the general conditions of your garden. Refer to a practical garden manual or plant reference directory for specific information on particular plants in your garden.

SPRING

Containers:

- *Plant new containers once the danger of frost has passed*
- *Remove any dead or unwanted growth from permanent container plants*
- *Replace the top 2 in (5cm) of soil with fresh potting compost*
- *Deal with any problems caused by pests or diseases immediately*

Beds and Borders:

- *Plant herbaceous perennials*
- *Sow seeds of annuals*
- *Fertilize and mulch flower beds and borders*
- *Cut back any dead or straggly growth from perennial plants*
- *Lift and divide large clumps of perennials*
- *Take cuttings of pot plants and summer bedding plants*
- *Prune roses*
- *Stake perennials*

Lawns:

- *Lay new turf or plant grass seed*
- *Fertilize the existing lawn*
- *Mow the lawn regularly and keep the edges trimmed*
- *Repair lawn edges and dips*
- *Remove lawn weeds*

Trees and Shrubs:

- *Plant container-grown trees and shrubs*
- *Prune winter-flowering shrubs*
- *Remove any dead or diseased stems*
- *In early spring, prune shrubs that flower after midsummer*
- *Trim and plant hedges*
- *Prune spring-flowering shrubs as soon as the flowers fade*
- *Plant bare-rooted deciduous trees or shrubs*

Water Gardens:

- *Add more water if necessary*
- *Plant new pond and marginal plants in late spring*
- *Remove algae and debris from the water*
- *Divide or replace overgrown plants in fresh soil*

Kitchen Gardens:

- *Sow seeds of annual herbs*
- *Remove straggly stems of woody herbs, such as rosemary*
- *Trim back small, bushy herbs to keep the plants compact*

SUMMER

Containers:

- *Water containers regularly, once or twice a day in high temperatures*
- *Deadhead flowers regularly to encourage new flowers*
- *Feed plants with liquid fertilizer regularly*
- *Plant hanging baskets and window boxes with summer bedding plants*

Beds and Borders:

- *Sow seeds of biennials*
- *Fertilize roses after first flowering*
- *Treat signs of pests and disease immediately*
- *Deadhead flowers regularly*
- *Water beds and borders regularly*
- *Hoe beds and borders to remove weeds*
- *Prune climbers that flower before midsummer*

Lawns:

- *Mow the lawn in dry weather, keep grass to a height of $\frac{1}{2}$–2 in (1–5 cm)*
- *Water when necessary, adding lawn feed following manufacturer's instructions*
- *Keep the lawn weed-free*
- *Keep lawn edges neatly-trimmed*
- *Cut down spring-flowering meadow once flowers have seeded*

Trees and Shrubs:

- *Prune trained trees and shrubs to maintain their shape*
- *Clip evergreen hedges and topiary with sharp shears or secateurs*
- *Layer trees and shrubs*

Water Gardens:

- *Maintain the level of water in the pond*
- *Remove water lily leaves that are pushing out of the water*
- *Remove algae or pond weed*
- *Keep soil in the pond margins moist*

Kitchen Gardens:

- *Pinch out new flowering shoots of herbs*
- *Clip bay trees*
- *Trim bushy herbs to maintain a compact shape*

FALL

Containers:

- *Plant spring-flowering bulbs and lilies*
- *Bring frost-tender perennials indoors*
- *Feed and water containers regularly*
- *Plant fall container plants*
- *Continue to deadhead flowers*

Beds and Borders:

- *Remove weeds regularly*
- *Plant winter- and spring-flowering bulbs and lilies*
- *Clear summer bedding*
- *Lift and divide herbaceous plants*
- *Cut down dead tops of perennials*
- *Sow hardy annuals for early flowers the following year*

Lawns:

- *Sow lawn seed or lay new turf*
- *Repair damaged areas*
- *Mow the lawn while the grass is still growing, keep to a height of $^3/_4$ in (2 cm)*
- *Plant spring-flowering bulbs into lawn*
- *Feed the lawn as required*

Trees and Shrubs:

- *Collect leaves for use as compost*
- *Plant bare root trees and shrubs*
- *Apply a layer of coarse mulch around trees and shrubs before the cold weather to insulate the soil*

Water Gardens:

- *Remove any frost-tender water plants to a frost-free place*
- *Remove any dead leaves from the surface of ponds*

Kitchen Gardens:

- *Divide mint plants that are overcrowded*
- *Tidy herb beds, removing dead growth*
- *Trim back shrubby herbs*

WINTER

Containers:

- *Discontinue watering plants*
- *Remove and discard dead bedding plants*
- *Clean empty pots in soapy water*
- *Position containers in a sheltered position over winter months*
- *Drain off rain water to keep plants relatively dry*
- *Bring vulnerable plants inside*

Beds and Borders:

- *Firm soil down around plants*
- *Cut back dead perennial stems*
- *Plan next year's plantings; order seeds and bulbs from catalogs*

Lawns:

- *Avoid walking on lawns in cold or damp weather as you can damage the soil*
- *Clean and service the lawnmower before winter storage*

Trees and Shrubs:

- *Collect leaves for compost*
- *Knock heavy falls of snow off hedges and branches*
- *Plant out bareroot trees, shrubs, and hedge plants*
- *Plant climbers*
- *Prune late-flowering summer shrubs*

Water Gardens:

- *Clean the pond pump filter*
- *If you have fish, make sure that there is a hole in the ice during freezing weather*

Kitchen Gardens:

- *Mulch established fruit trees*
- *Insulate cold frames against frost*

Plant List

The following list details a selection of plants suitable for particular sites and purposes. If several species and varieties within a genus are suitable, then only the genus has been listed. Specific varieties have been given where they offer individual characteristics. Always check that the plant is suitable for your conditions before purchasing.

KEY

a	annual and biennial
al	alpine
a/p	tender perennial treated as annual
b	bulb, corm, stolon, or tuber
c	climber
c/s	cactus/succulent
e	evergreen
p	perennial
s	shrub
t	tree
wp	water plant

THE CONTAINED GARDEN

Good container plants

Acer palmatum 'Bloodgood' [t]
Agapanthus spp. and cvs (African lily) [a/p]
Anemone nemorosa (wood anemone) [b]
Argyranthemum spp. and cvs (marguerite daisy) [a/p]
Bougainvillea spp. and cvs [c, e]
Brugmansia spp. and cvs (angel's trumpet) [a/p]
Buxus sempervirens cvs (box) [s]
Cineraria spp. and cvs [p]
Fuchsia spp. and cvs [s]
Hebe spp. and cvs [e, s]
Hedera spp. and cvs (ivy) [c, e]
Helichrysum petiolare [a/p]
Hosta spp. and cvs [p]
Hyacinthus orientalis cvs (hyacinth) [b]
Jasminum polyanthum (jasmine) [c, s]
Lathyrus odoratus (sweet pea) [a, c, p]
Laurus nobilis (sweet bay) [e, t]
Lavatera trimestris (mallow) [a]
Ligustrum spp. and cvs (privet) [e, s]
Lilium spp. and cvs [b]
Lobelia erinus (trailing lobelia) [a/p]
Narcissus spp. and cvs (daffodil) [b]
Pelargonium spp. and cvs [a/p]
Petunia spp. and cvs [a/p]
Philadelphus microphyllus (dwarf mock orange) [s]
Phyllostachys nigra (black bamboo) [e, s]
Primula spp. and cvs (primrose) [p]
Rosa 'Anna Pavlova' [s]
 R. 'Empereur du Maroc' [s]
Tropaeolum majus (nasturtium) [a]
Tulipa spp. and cvs (tulip) [b]
Viola x *wittrockiana* (pansy) [a]

Plants for hanging baskets

Bidens ferulifolia [a/p]
Convolvulus sabatius [a/p]
Diascia spp. and cvs [a]
Felicia amelloides [a/p]
Fuchsia 'Jack Shahan' [s]
Impatiens spp. and cvs (busy Lizzie) [a]
Verbena spp. and cvs [a]

Foliage container plants

Actinidia kolomikta [c]
Agave spp. and cvs [p]
Anthriscus sylvestris 'Moonlit Night' (cow parsley) [p]
Arundinaria falconeri (bamboo) [p]
Arundo donax (giant reed) [p]
Astelia nervosa [p]
Carex spp. and cvs [p]
Cedrus deodora 'Gold Mound' (cedar) [e, t]
Chamaecyparis pisifera 'Filifera Aurea' (false cypress) [e, t]
Choisya ternata (Mexican orange blossom) [e,s]
Cordyline spp. and cvs [p]
Cornus controversa (wedding cake tree) [t]
Euonymus fortunei 'Silver Queen' [e, s]
Euphorbia rigida (spurge) [e, p]
Garrya elliptica 'James Roof' [e, s]
Juniperus communis 'Compressa' [e, t]
Lamium maculatum (deadnettle) [p]
Leymus arenarius (lyme grass) [p]
Oxalis triangularis 'Cupido' (clover) [p]
Prunus lusitanica (Portugal laurel) [e, s]
Salvia officinalis (sage) [s]
 S. o. 'Purpurescens' (purple sage) [e, s]
Spiraea spp. and cvs [s]
Taxus spp. and cvs (yew) [e, s]

Color for containers

Reds, yellows, and oranges

Abutilon spp. and cvs [p]
Auricula spp. and cvs [p]
Begonia spp. and cvs [b]
Callistemon spp. and cvs (bottlebrush) [s]
Canna spp. and cvs (canna lily) [b]
Cheiranthus spp. and cvs (wallflower) [a]
Chrysanthemum spp. and cvs [a/p]
Clianthus puniceus (parrot's bill) [c, e]
Cosmos atrosanguineus [b]
Crocosmia spp. and cvs [b]
Dahlia cvs [b]
Hydrangea spp. and cvs [s]
Lilium 'Citronella' [b]
Mahonia spp. and cvs [e, s]

Pinks, blues, and purples

Ageratum spp. and cvs (floss flower) [a]
Anemone coronaria [b]
Cosmos spp. and cvs [a]
Cynara cardunculus (cardoon) [p]
Dianthus spp. and cvs [a, p]
Dipsacus fullonum (teasel) [a]
Eryngium spp. and cvs (sea holly) [p]
Helleborus spp. and cvs [p]
Hypoestes cv. (polka-dot-plant) [a/p]
Muscari spp. and cvs (grape hyacinth) [b]
Myosotis spp. and cvs (forget-me-not) [a, p]
Nicotiana spp. and cvs (tobacco plant) [a, p]
Origanum laevigatum (dittany) [p]

White

Clematis marmoraria (dwarf clematis) [e, s]
Dicentra spp. and cvs [p]
Lilium candidum (Madonna lily) [b]
Yucca recurvifolia [e, s]

Seasonal container plants

Spring

Crocus spp. and cvs [b]
Erythronium spp. and cvs (dog's tooth violet) [b]
Fritillaria imperialis (crown imperial) [b]
 F. michailovskyi (fritillary) [b]
Hyacinthus 'L'Innocence' (hyacinth) [b]
Iris bucharica (Juno iris) [b]
 I. magnifica (Juno iris) [b]
Narcissus 'February Gold' [b]
Tulipa 'Fancy Frills' [b]
Viola spp. and cvs [p]

Summer

Artemisia spp. and cvs (wormwood) [p]
Browallia speciosa [p]
Calendula officinalis (pot marigold) [a]
Geranium spp. and cvs [p]
Gloriosa superba 'Rothschildiana'
    (glory lily) [b]
Kalanchoe cvs [p]
Lathyrus odoratus (sweet pea) [a, c, p]
Lilium longiflorum (Easter lily) [b]
Malva sylvestris 'Primley Blue' [p]
Melianthus major [p]
Osteospermum 'Whirligig' [a/p]
Rosa cvs [s]
Tagetes spp. and cvs (African marigolds) [a]

Fall

Acer spp. and cvs (Japanese maple) [t]
Callicarpa bodinieri 'Profusion' [s]
Cotoneaster horizontalis [s]
Rosa virginiana [s]

Winter

Corylus avellana 'Contorta'
    (corkscrew hazel) [t]
Crocus laevigatus 'Fontenayi'
    C. x *luteus* (Dutch yellow crocus) [b]
    C. tommasinianus albus [b]
    C. t. 'Barr's Purple' [b]
Cyclamen coum cvs [b]
    C. persicum cvs [b]
Eranthis hyemalis (winter aconite) [b]
Galanthus spp. and cvs (snowdrop) [b]
Skimmia japonica 'Tansley Gem' [e, s]

Specialty plants

Alpine plants
Campanula garganica 'Dickson's Gold' [p]
Sedum spathulifolium 'Purpureum'
    (stonecrop) [p]
Sempervivum ssp. and cvs (houseleek) [p]

Herbs
Artemisia ssp. and cvs (wormwood) [p]
Ocimum ssp. and cvs (basil) [a]
Petroselinum ssp. and cvs (parsley) [a]
Rosmarinus officinalis (rosemary) [s]
Tanacetum parthenium (golden feverfew) [a/p]
    T. vulgare (tansy) [p]
Thymus spp. and cvs (thyme) [e, s]

Scented plants
Citrus spp. and cvs
    (lemon, orange, kumquat) [s]

Daphne bholua 'Jacqueline Postill' [e, s]
    D. odora 'Aureomarginata' [e, s]
Freesia cvs [b]
Gladiolus callianthus 'Murieliae' [b]
Heliotropium spp. and cvs (heliotrope) [a]
Hoya spp. and cvs [e, p]
Lavandula latifolia (upright lavender) [e, s]

THE GARDEN IN BLOOM

Good border plants

Achillea spp. and cvs (yarrow) [p]
Agapanthus spp. and cvs (African lily) [b]
Alchemilla mollis (lady's mantle) [p]
Anemone x *hybrida* (Japanese anemone) [p]
Artemisia spp. and cvs (wormwood) [p]
Aster novae-angliae spp. and cvs
    (Michaelmas daisy) [p]
    A. novi-belgii spp. and cvs [p]
Astilbe spp. and cvs [p]
Bergenia spp. and cvs (elephant's ears) [p]
Buxus sempervirens cvs (box) [s]
Camellia spp. and cvs [e, s]
Centaurea cyanus (cornflower) [a]
Centranthus ruber (red valerian) [p]
Cheiranthus spp. and cvs (wallflowers) [a]
Clematis spp. and cvs [c]
Cortaderia spp. and cvs (pampas grass) [p]
Crambe cordifolia [p]
Dahlia cvs [b]
Daphne spp. and cvs [e, s]
Delphinium spp. and cvs [p]
Dianthus spp. and cvs (pink) [a, p]
Erigeron spp. and cvs (fleabane) [p]
Eryngium pandanifolium (sea holly) [p]
Euphorbia spp. and cvs (spurge) [p]
Fuchsia spp. and cvs [s]
Genista spp. and cvs (broom) [s]
Geranium spp. and cvs [p]
Geum spp. and cvs [p]
Gypsophila spp. and cvs [p]
Helenium spp. and cvs (sneezeweed) [p]
Helianthemum spp. and cvs (sunflower) [a, p]
Juniperus spp. and cvs (juniper) [s, t]
Kniphofia spp. and cvs (red-hot poker) [p]
Lathyrus odoratus (sweet pea) [a, c, p]
Lavandula spp. and cvs (lavender) [s]
Lavatera spp. and cvs
    (mallow, tree mallow) [a, p]
Leucanthemum spp. and cvs (marguerite) [p]
Liatris spp. and cvs (blazing star) [p]
Lobelia spp. and cvs [p]
Lupinus spp. and cvs (lupin) [p]
Macleaya spp. and cvs (plume poppy) [p]

Malus floribunda (crab apple) [t]
Miscanthus sinensis (silver grass) [p]
Myosotis spp. and cvs (forget-me-not) [a]
Nepeta spp. and cvs (catmint) [p]
Paeonia spp. and cvs (peony) [p]
Papaver spp. and cvs (poppy) [a, p]
Phlomis anatolica (Jerusalem sage) [s]
Phlox spp. and cvs [p]
Phormium spp. and cvs [p]
Photinia villosa [s]
Rhododendron spp. and cvs [e, s]
Rhus spp. and cvs (sumach) [s, t]
Rosa spp. and cvs [c, s]
Sedum spectabile cvs (ice plant) [p]
Tulipa spp. and cvs (tulip) [b]
Verbena bonariensis [p]
Viola x *wittrockiana* (pansy) [a]

Ground cover and edging plants

Anthemis punctata ssp. *cupaniana*
    (marguerite) [p]
Asperula odorata (sweet woodruff) [p]
Aubrieta spp. and cvs [p]
Campanula poscharskyana
    (spreading bellflower) [p]
Corydalis spp. and cvs [p]
Dimorphotheca spp. and cvs
    (Cape marigold) [a/p]
Iris pseudacorus cvs (flag iris) [b]
Lamium spp. and cvs (deadnettle) [p]
Petunia spp. and cvs [a]
Pyrethrum (pyrethrum daisy) [p]
Rudbeckia spp. and cvs [p]
Symphytum grandiflorum (dwarf comfrey) [p]
Viola tricolor (heartsease) [p]

Plants for the back of the border

Alcea spp. and cvs (hollyhock) [p]
Clematis alpina cvs [c]
    C. florida 'Seiboldii' [c]
    C. 'Fuji-musume' [c]
    C. 'Madame Julia Correvon' [c]
    C. montana cvs [c]
    C. 'Pink Fantasy' [c]
Echinops ritro (globe thistle) [p]
Foeniculum vulgare 'Purpureum'
    (bronze fennel) [p]
Lonicera spp. and cvs (honeysuckle) [c, s]
Tropaeolum perigrinum (canary creeper) [a, c]

Trees and shrubs

Abies koreana (Korean fir) [e, t]
Acer spp. and cvs (maple) [t]
Arbutus spp. and cvs (strawberry tree) [e, s, t]

Calluna spp. and cvs [e, s]

Carpinus betulus 'Fastigiata' (hornbeam) spp.
and cvs [c, e, s]

Catalpa bignonioides (Indian bean tree) [t]

Cedrus atlantica 'Glauca' (blue cedar) [t]

Corylus maxima 'Purpurea'
(purple leaf hazel) [t]

Cryptomeria japonica 'Elegans Aurea' [e, t]

Cupressus sempervirens 'Swane's Gold'
(cypress) [e, t]

Erica spp. and cvs [e, s]

Euonymus spp. and cvs [e, s]

Hebe spp. and cvs [e, s]

Helichrysum italicum (curry plant) [p]

Ilex spp. and cvs (holly) [e, s, t]

Magnolia spp. and cvs [t]

Potentilla fruticosa 'Primrose Beauty' [s]

Pyrus communis var. *sativa* (pear) [t]

Quercus spp. and cvs (oak) [t]

Rosa 'Charles Rennie Macintosh' [s]
R. 'Graham Thomas' [s]
R. 'Mary Rose' [s]
R. *gallica versicolor* ('Rosa Mundi') [s]

Rosmarinus officinalis (rosemary) [s]

Santolina spp. and cvs (cotton lavender) [e, s]

Spiraea spp. and cvs [e, s]

Styrax japonicus (Japanese snowbell) [t]

Taxus spp. and cvs (yew) [e, s, t]

Thuja plicata (Western red cedar) [e, t]

Flowering shrubs

Ceanothus spp. and cvs
(Californian lilac) [c, e, s]

Daphne acutiloba [e, s]

Fuschia spp. and cvs [s]

Heliotropium arborescens 'Marine' [e, s]

Hydrangea spp. and cvs [s]

Rhododendron spp. and cvs [e, s]

Skimmia japonica cvs [e, s]

Viburnum tinus (laurustinus) [e, s]

Variegated and silver plants

Aegopodium podagraria 'Variegatum'
(variegated ground elder) [p]

Berberis sp. and cvs [s]

Convolvulus cneorum [s]

Cornus sp. and cvs (dogwood) [s]

Cotoneaster atropurpureus 'Variegatus' [s]

Euonymus fortunei 'Emerald 'n' Gold' [e, s]
E. f. 'Harlequin' [e, s]

Hedera colchica 'Dentata Variegata' (ivy) [c, e]

Hosta fortunei var. *aureomarginata* [p]

Ilex aquifolium 'Silver Queen' (holly) [e, s]

Lychnis coronaria cvs [p]

Matthiola incana cvs (perpetual stock) [p]

Mentha suaveolens 'Variegata' (apple mint) [p]

Santolina chamaecyparissus (cotton lavender) [s]

Senecio 'Sunshine' [s]

Weigela spp. and cvs [s]

Perennials

Aconitum spp. and cvs (monkshood) [p]

Alcea spp. and cvs (hollyhock) [p]

Anchusa spp. and cvs [p]

Aquilegia spp. and cvs (columbine, granny's
bonnet) [p]

Aster spp. and cvs [p]

A. novi-belgii spp. and cvs [p]

Astrantia spp. and cvs (masterwort) [p]

Brunnera spp. and cvs [p]

Centaurea spp. and cvs
(cornflower, knapweed) [p]

Crinum spp. and cvs (crinum lily) [b]

Dicentra spp. and cvs (bleeding heart) [p]

Digitalis spp. and cvs (foxgloves) [p]

Doronicum spp. and cvs (leopard's bane) [p]

Echinacea spp. and cvs (purple coneflower) [p]

Eupatorium spp. and cvs (Joe-Pye weed) [p]

Festuca glauca (blue grass) [p]

Hosta spp. and cvs [p]

Knautia macedonica [p]

Kniphofia spp. and cvs (red-hot poker) [p]

Ligularia spp. and cvs [p]

Lychnis coronaria cvs [p]

Meconopsis betonicifolia (Himalayan
blue poppy) [p]
M. *cambrica* (Welsh poppy) [p]

Papaver orientale (oriental poppy) [p]
P. o. 'Curlilocks' [p]
P. o. 'Perry's White' [p]
P. *somniferum* (opium poppy) [p]

Penstemon spp. and cvs [p]

Physostegia spp. and cvs (obedient plant) [p]

Polygonatum spp. and cvs (Solomon's seal) [b]

Pulmonaria spp. and cvs (lungwort) [p]

Rudbeckia spp. and cvs (coneflower) [p]

Salvia involucrata 'Bethellii' [p]
S. *nemorosa* [p]
S. *patens* [p]

Solidago spp. and cvs (golden rod) [p]

Verbascum spp. and cvs (mullein) [p]

Viola cornuta cvs (horned pansy) [p]

Annuals and bulbs, corms and tubers

Allium spp. and cvs [b]

Amaranthus spp. and cvs (love-lies-bleeding) [a]

Antirrhinum spp. and cvs (snapdragon) [a]

Calendula officinalis cvs (pot marigold) [a]

Callistephus chinensis cvs (China aster) [a]

Campanula media cvs (Canterbury bell) [a]

Chionodoxa forbesii spp. and cvs
(glory of the snow) [b]

Clarkia spp. and cvs [a]

Coreopsis spp. and cvs (tickseed) [a]

Cosmos spp. and cvs [a]

Crinum spp. and cvs (crinum lily) [b]

Crocosmia spp. and cvs [b]

Crocus spp. and cvs [b]

Dahlia cvs [b]

Dianthus barbatus (sweet William) [a]

Eschscholzia spp. and cvs
(Californian poppy) [a]

Gaillardia spp. and cvs [a]

Gladioli spp. and cvs [b]

Hyacinthoides non-scripta cvs (bluebell) [b]

Hyacinthus orientalis cvs (hyacinth) [b]

Iris spp. and cvs [b]

Lavatera spp. and cvs (blazing star) [a]

Lilium spp. and cvs [b]

Lunaria annua cvs (honesty) [a]

Matthiola spp. and cvs (stock) [a]

Muscari spp. and cvs (grape hyacinth) [a]

Narcissus spp. and cvs (daffodil) [b]

Nemesia strumosa Carnival Series [a]

Nicotiana spp. and cvs (tobacco plant) [a]
N. *sylvestris* [a]

Nigella spp. and cvs (love-in-a-mist) [a]

Petunia spp. and cvs [a]

Scilla siberica spp. and cvs (squill) [b]

Sternbergia spp. and cvs [b]

Tagetes spp. and cvs
(African and French marigold) [a]

Tulipa spp. and cvs (tulip) [b]

Tropaeolum spp. and cvs (nasturtium) [a]

Viola x *wittrockiana* (pansy) [a]

Zinnia spp. and cvs [a]

Plants for color
Hot colors

Acacia dealbata (mimosa) [t]

Achillea filipendulina 'Gold Plate' [p]

Antirrhinum spp. and cvs (snapdragon) [a]

Beta vulgaris 'Rhubarb Chard'
(red-stemmed chard) [a]

Chrysanthemum spp. and cvs [p]

Coreopsis tinctoria (tickseed) [a]

Cornus spp. and cvs [s]

Crocosmia spp. and cvs [b]

Dianthus cvs (carnation) [a]

Hemerocallis spp. and cvs (day lily) [p]

Heuchera micrantha 'Palace Purple' [p]

Kniphofia spp. and cvs (red-hot poker) [p]

Lilium spp. and cvs (lily) [p]
Lupinus spp. and cvs (lupin) [p]
Lychnis chalcedonica (Jerusalem cross) [p]
Lysimachia spp. and cvs [p]
Narcissus spp. and cvs (daffodil) [b]
Papaver spp. and cvs (poppy) [a, p]
Rudbeckia spp. and cvs [p]
Solidago spp. and cvs (golden rod) [p]
Tagetes spp. and cvs
    (African and French marigold) [a]
Tropaeolum spp. and cvs (nasturtium) [a]
Tulipa spp. and cvs (tulip) [b]
Verbascum spp. and cvs (mullein) [p]

Cool colors
Agapanthus spp. and cvs (African lily) [b]
Allium aflatunense (ornamental onion) [b]
    A. sphaerocephalon [b]
Anchusa spp. and cvs [p]
Aquilegia vulgaris (columbine,
    granny's bonnet) [p]
Campanula spp. and cvs (bellflower) [p]
Ceanothus spp. and cvs
    (Californian lilac) [c, e, s]
Clematis alpina 'Frances Rivis' [c]
    C. jackmanii [c]
Delphinium spp. and cvs [p]
Eranthis hyemalis (winter aconite) [b]
Hetercentron elegans [p]
Hosta 'Buckshaw Blue' [p]
    H. sieboldiana [p]
Hyacinthus orientalis cvs (hyacinth) [b]
Hydrangea spp. and cvs [s]
Iris spp. and cvs [b]
    I. sibirica 'Perry's Blue' [b]
Lamium maculatum (deadnettle) [p]
Lewisia cotyledon [p]
Linum perenne (blue flax) [p]
Penstemon spp. and cvs [p]
Rosa 'Ferdinand Pichard' [s]
    R. gallica versicolor ('Rosa Mundi') [s]
    R. glauca [s]
    R. 'The Fairy' [s]
Scilla siberica spp. and cvs (squill) [b]
Syringa spp. and cvs (lilac) [t]
Thalictrum spp. and cvs (meadow rue) [p]
Trachelium caeruleum (throatwort) [p]

White and green
Acanthus spp. and cvs (bear's breeches) [p]
Alcea rosea cvs (hollyhock) [p]
Anemone x hybrida 'Honorine Jobert'
    (Japanese anemone) [p]
Asperula odorata (sweet woodruff) [p]
Astrantia spp. and cvs (masterwort) [p]

Celmisia hookeri [p]
Cornus alba 'Elegantissima' [s]
Digitalis spp. and cvs (foxglove) [a, p]
Euphorbia characias ssp. *wulfenii* [e, p]
Foeniculum vulgare 'Purpureum'
    (bronze fennel) [p]
Fritillaria pontica (fritillary) [b]
    F. verticillata (fritillary) [b]
Galanthus spp. and cvs (snowdrop) [b]
Galega officinalis 'Alba' (goat's rue) [p]
Hosta spp. and cvs [p]
Hydrangea spp. and cvs [s]
Iris pallida 'Variegata' [b]
Lychnis coronaria 'Alba' [p]
Molucella laevis (bells of Ireland) [a]
Narcissus spp. and cvs (daffodil) [b]
Nicotiana 'Lime Green' [a]
Phormium spp. and cvs [e, s]
Pittosporum spp. and cvs [e, s]
Polygonatum spp. and
    (Solomon's seal) [b]
Rodgersia aesculifolia [p]
Rosa chinensis 'Viridiflora' (green rose) [s]
Smyrnium perfoliatum [p]
Viburnum opulus (geulder rose) [s]

GARDEN STYLE
Good garden plants
Acer spp. and cvs (maple) [t]
Agapanthus spp. and cvs (African lily) [b]
Alcea spp. and cvs (hollyhock) [a/p]
Alchemilla mollis (lady's mantle) [p]
Antirrhinum spp. and cvs (snapdragon) [a]
Aquilegia spp. and cvs (columbine,
    granny's bonnet) [p]
Arundinaria spp. and cvs (bamboo) [s]
Aster novae-angliae spp. and cvs
    (Michaelmas daisy) [p]
    A. novi-belgii spp. and cvs [p]
Bougainvillea spp. and cvs [c, e]
Buxus sempervirens cvs (box) [e, s]
Calendula officinalis (pot marigold) [a]
Cheiranthus spp. and cvs (wallflower) [a]
Chimonanthus praecox (wintersweet) [s]
Choisya ternata (Mexican orange
    blossom) [e, s]
Clarkia cvs [a]
Clematis spp. and cvs [c, p]
Crocus spp. and cvs [b]
Fuchsia spp. and cvs [s]
Galanthus spp. and cvs (snowdrop) [b]
Geum spp. and cvs [p]
Gloriosa superba (glory lily) [b]
Hebe spp. and cvs [s]

Hedera spp. and cvs (ivy) [c, e]
Hyacinthus orientalis cvs (hyacinth) [b]
Iris spp. and cvs [b]
Jasminum spp. and cvs (jasmine) [c, s]
Laurus nobilis (sweet bay) [e, t]
Lavandula spp. and cvs (lavender) [s]
Lilium spp. and cvs [b]
Lonicera spp. and cvs (honeysuckle) [c]
Muscari spp. and cvs (grape hyacinth) [b]
Nigella damascena (love-in-a-mist) [a]
Pelargonium spp. and cvs [a/p]
Petunia spp. and cvs [a]
Phyllostachys spp. and cvs (bamboo) [e, s]
Rudbeckia spp. and cvs (coneflower) [p]
Santolina chamaecyparissus (cotton lavender) [s]
Solidago spp. and cvs (golden rod) [p]
Taxus baccata (yew) [e, s]
Tropaeolum majus (nasturtium) [a]
Tulipa spp. and cvs (tulip) [b]
Verbena spp. and cvs [a]

Plants for paving and paths
Ajuga reptans (bugle) [p]
Chamaemelum nobile (chamomile) [p]
Dianthus spp. and cvs (pink) [a, p]
Meconopsis cambrica (Welsh poppy) [p]
Mentha requienii (Corsican mint) [p]
Thymus serpyllum (creeping thyme) [e, p]
Viola odorata cvs (sweet violet) [p]
    V. tricolor cvs (heartsease) [p]

Climbing plants for arches, walls, and trellises
Ceanothus spp. and cvs (Californian lilac)
    [c, e, s]
Cissus rhombifolia (grape ivy) [c]
Clematis spp. and cvs [c]
Hedera helix 'Arborescens' (ivy) [c, e]
Humulus lupulus 'Aureus' (golden hop) [c, p]
Parthenocissus henryana (Virgina creeper) [c]
Passiflora caerulea (passion flower) [c]
Solanum crispum 'Glasnevin' (potato vine) [c]
Wisteria cvs [c]

Trees and hedging plants
Crataegus spp. and cvs (hawthorn) [t]
Elaeagnus x ebbingei [e, s]
Fagus sylvatica (beech) [t]
Ilex spp. and cvs (holly) [e, t]
Ligustrum ovalifolium (oval-leaved privet) [s]
Mahonia x media 'Charity' [e, s]
Taxus baccata (yew) [e, s]
Thuja plicata (Western red cedar) [e, t]

Plants for focal points

Allium spp. and cvs (ornamental onion) [b]
   A. giganteum [b]
Amelanchier lamarckii (snowy mespilus) [t]
Catalpa bignonioides (Indian bean tree)
Cynara scolymus (globe artichoke) [p]
Fagus sylvatica 'Pendula' (weeping beech) [t]
Foeniculum vulgare 'Purpureum'
   (bronze fennel) [p]
Laburnum spp. and cvs [t]
Liquidamber styraciflua (sweet gum) [t]
Mahonia x *media* 'Charity' [e, s]
Malus x *zumi* 'Golden Hornet' (crab apple) [t]
Miscanthus spp. and cvs (silver grass) [p]

Seasonal interest

Winter

Cornus spp. and cvs (dogwood) [s]
Eranthis hyemalis (winter aconite) [b]
Euonymus fortunei 'Emerald 'n' Gold' [e, s]
Galanthus spp. and cvs (snowdrop) [b]
Helleborus spp. and cvs (hellebore) [p]
Ilex spp. and cvs (holly) [t]
Mahonia x *media* 'Charity' [e, s]
Picea spp. and cvs (spruce) [t]
Skimmia japonica [e, s]
Stachyurus praecox [e, s]
Viburnum tinus (laurustinus) [e, s]

Spring

Cheiranthus spp. and cvs (wallflower) [a]
Crocus spp. and cvs [b]
Forsythia spp. and cvs [s]
Fritillaria meleagris (crown imperial) [b]
Lobularia maritima (white alyssum) [a]
Myosotis spp. and cvs (forget-me-not) [a, p]
Narcissus spp. and cvs (daffodil) [b]
Philadelphus spp. and cvs (mock orange) [s]
Primula spp. and cvs (primrose, polyanthus) [p]
Prunus spp. and cvs (ornamental,
   flowering cherry) [t]
Tulipa spp. and cvs (tulip) [b]

Summer to fall

Acanthus spp. and cvs (bear's breeches) [p]
Aconitum spp. and cvs (monkshood) [p]
Delphinium spp. and cvs [p]
Helenium 'Crimson Beauty' (sneezeweed) [p]
Helianthus annuus (annual sunflower) [a]
Lilium spp. and cvs [b]
Osteospermum spp. and cvs [a/p]
Papaver orientale (oriental poppy) [p]
Pelargonium spp. and cvs [a/p]
Rudbeckia spp. and cvs (coneflower) [p]

Plants for sunny sites

Agave spp. and cvs [c/s]
Allium spp. and cvs (ornamental onion) [b]
Ballota spp. and cvs [p]
Cistus spp. and cvs (rock rose) [s]
Cytisus spp. and cvs (broom) [s]
Echinacea purpurea cvs
   (purple coneflower) [p]
Erigeron glaucus (fleabane) [al]
Erinus alpinus [al]
Eschscholzia spp. and cvs (Californian
   poppy) [a]
Genista spp. and cvs (broom) [s]
Linum arboreum (flax) [al]
Osteospermum spp. and cvs [a/p]
Rosmarinus officinalis (rosemary) [s]
Salvia spp. and cvs (sage) [s]
Sedum spp. and cvs (ice plant, stonecrop) [p]
Sempervivum spp. and cvs (houseleek) [p]
Stachys byzantina (lamb's ears) [p]
Thymus spp. and cvs (thyme) [e, p]

Plants for shady sites

Cyclamen spp. and cvs [b]
Digitalis Excelsior Group (foxglove) [a/p]
Elaeagnus spp. and cvs [e, s]
Epimedium spp. and cvs [p]
Erythronium spp. and cvs
   (dog's tooth violet) [b]
Euonymus fortunei cvs [e, s]
Geranium spp. and cvs (hardy geranium) [p]
Helleborus spp. and cvs [p]
   H. argutifolius (Corsican hellebore) [p]
Hosta spp. and cvs [p]
Hyacinthoides non-scripta cvs (bluebell) [b]
Hypericum spp. and cvs (St John's wort) [p, s]
Lythrum spp. and cvs (purple loosestrife) [p]
Melissa officinalis (lemon balm) [p]
Myosotis spp. and cvs (forget-me-not) [a, p]
Myrrhis odorata (sweet cicely) [p]
Paeonia spp. and cvs (peony) [p]
Polypodium vulgare (polypody fern) [p]
Primula spp. and cvs (primrose) [p]
Pulmonaria rubra (lungwort) [p]
Soleirolia soleirolii (mind-your-
   own-business) [p]

GARDEN THEMES

Cottage garden plants

Alcea rosea (hollyhock) [a, p]
Campanula spp. and cvs (bellflower) [a]
Centaurea cyanus (cornflower) [a]
Consolida ajacis (larkspur) [a/p]
Delphinium spp. and cvs [p]

Digitalis spp. (foxglove) [a, p]
Erigeron karvinskianus (fleabane) [p]
Lathyrus spp. (sweet pea) [a, c, p]
Lavatera trimestris (mallow) [a]
Matthiola spp. and cvs (stock) [a, p]
Rosa ssp. and cvs [s]
Salvia viridis (clary sage) [a/p]
Stachys byzantina (lamb's ears) [p]
Verbascum spp. and cvs (mullein) [p]

Fragrant flowers

Convallaria majalis (lily-of-the-valley) [p]
Cytisus battandieri (pineapple broom) [s]
Daphne spp. and cvs [s]
Dianthus spp. and cvs (pink) [p]
Helichrysum italicum (curry plant) [p]
Heliotropium spp. and cvs (heliotrope) [a]
Jasminum officinale (jasmine) [c, s]
Lathyrus odoratus (sweet pea) [a, c]
Lavandula spp. and cvs (lavender) [p]
Lilium spp. and cvs (lily) [b]
Lonicera periclymenum (honeysuckle) [c, s]
Matthiola bicornis (night-scented stock) [a]
Oenothera spp. and cvs (evening primrose) [a,p]
Philadelphus spp. and cvs (mock orange) [s]
Rosa 'Crépuscule' [s]
Syringa spp. and cvs (lilac) [t]
Viburnum spp. and cvs [s]

Flowers for cutting

Alchemilla mollis (lady's mantle) [p]
Aquilegia spp. and cvs (columbine,
   granny's bonnet) [p]
Calendula officinalis (marigold) [a]
Cynara cardunculus (cardoon) [p]
Dahlia cvs [b]
Daphne spp. and cvs [e, s]
Delphinium ssp. and cvs [p]
Forsythia spp. and cvs [s]
Geranium spp. and cvs [p]
Helleborus niger (Christmas rose) [p]
Iris xiphium hybrids (Dutch iris) [b]
Lilium spp. and cvs (lily) [b]
Myosotis spp. and cvs (forget-me-not) [a, p]
Nigella damescena (love-in-a-mist) [a]
Paeonia spp. and cvs (peony) [p]
Philadelphus spp. and cvs (mock orange) [s]
Ranunculus spp. and cvs (buttercup) [p]
Rosa ssp. and cvs [s]
Tulipa spp. and cvs (tulip) [b]

Plants for water and bog gardens

Acorus gramineus 'Variegatus' (sweet flag) [wp]
Caltha palustris (marsh marigold) [wp]
Canna glauca [b]

Darmera peltatum (syn. *Peltiphyllum peltatum*) (umbrella plant) [wp]
Dierama pulcherrimum (angel's fishing rod) [b]
Eriophorum angustifolium (cotton grass) [p]
Geum rivale (water avens) [wp]
Hemerocallis 'Stella de Oro' (day lily) [p]
Iris delavayi [b]
   I. ensata Higo hybrids (Japanese water iris) [b]
   I. laevigatae [b]
   I. pallida (great purple flag) [b]
   I. pseudacorus (yellow flag) [b, wp]
   I. p. x *versicolor* (blue flag) [b, wp]
Ligularia spp. and cvs [p]
Lysichiton americanus (bog arum) [p]
Mentha aquatica (water mint) [wp]
Nymphaea alba (white water lily) [wp]
   N. 'Sunrise' (syn *N.* 'Odorata Sulphurea Grandiflora') (water lily) [wp]
Pontederia cordata (pickerel weed) [wp]
Primula spp. and cvs (candelabra primula) [p]
Rheum spp. and cvs (giant rhubarb) [p]
Rodgersia spp. and cvs [p]
Typha minima (dwarf cat's tail) [wp]

Plants for dry sites
Aeonium arboreum 'Zwartkop' [c/s]
Allium spp. and cvs (ornamental onion) [b]
Armeria (thrift) [e, p]
Carnegiea gigantea [c/s]
Echeveria spp. and cvs [c/s]
Eryngium spp. and cvs (sea holly) [p]
   E. agavifolium [p]
Euphorbia spp. and cvs (spurge) [e, p]
Fargesia murieliae 'Simba' (bamboo) [e, s]
Geranium 'Ann Folkard' [p]
Hebe spp. and cvs [e, s]
Hordeum jubatum (foxtail grass) [a/p]
Opuntia (prickly pear) [c/s]
Sempervivum spp. and cvs [c/s]
Stipa gigantea [p]
Thymus spp. and cvs (thyme) [e, s]
Yucca gloriosa (Spanish dagger) [e, s]
   Y. whipplei [e, s]

Flowers for shade
Anemone nemorosa (wood anemone) [b]
Arum italicum (arum lily) [b]
Cyclamen coum cvs [b]
   C. hederifolium cvs [b]
Digitalis spp. and cvs (foxglove) [a, p]
Erythronium spp. and cvs (dog's tooth violet) [b]
Galanthus spp. and cvs (snowdrop) [b]

Hedera spp. and cvs (ivy) [c. e]
Helleborus spp. and cvs [p]
Hosta spp. and cvs [p]
Hyacinthoides non-scripta cvs (bluebell) [b]
Hydrangea spp. and cvs [s]
Laburnum spp. and cvs [t]
Lunaria annua (honesty) [a]
Myosotis spp. and cvs (forget-me-not) [a]
Polygonatum spp. and cvs (Solomon's seal) [b]
Primula spp. and cvs (primula) [p]
   P. vulgaris (primrose) [p]
Pulmonaria spp. and cvs (lungwort) [p]
Rhododendron spp. and cvs [e, s]
Rosa 'Madame Alfred Carrière' [s]
   R. canina (briar rose, dog rose) [c]
Sambucus niger (black elder) [t]
Sisyrinchium spp. and cvs [p]
Trillium spp. and cvs [p]
Vinca major (greater periwinkle) [e, p]
Viola odorata (sweet violet) [p]

Wildflowers for meadow areas
Anthriscus sylvestris (cow parsley) [p]
Centaurea cyanus (cornflower) [a]
Chamaemelum nobile (chamomile) [p]
Leucanthemum vulgare (ox-eye daisy) [p]
Lychnis flos-cuculi (ragged robin) [p]
Malva moschata (musk mallow) [p]
Papaver rhoeas (corn poppy) [a]
Polemonium spp. and cvs (Jacob's ladder) [p]
Ranunculus spp. and cvs (buttercup) [p]
Silene dioica (campion) [p]
Verbascum spp. and cvs (mullein) [p]
Viola tricolor (heartsease) [p]

Plants for attracting wildlife
Achillea spp. and cvs (yarrow) [p]
Asclepias spp. and cvs (milkweed) [p]
Aster novi-belgii (Michaelmas daisy) [p]
Buddleja spp. and cvs (butterfly bush) [s]
Corylus spp. and cvs (hazel) [t]
Eupatorium spp. and cvs (Joe-Pye weed) [p]
Euphorbia spp. and cvs (spurge) [e, p]
Fagus spp. and cvs (beech) [t]
Fritillaria spp. and cvs (fritillary) [b]
Ilex spp. and cvs (holly) [t]
Leucanthemum x *superbum* (shasta daisy) [p]
Lychnis flos-cuculi (ragged robin) [p]
Nymphaea spp. and cvs (water lily) [wp]
Papaver spp. and cvs (poppy) [p]
Phacelia tanacetifolium (Californian bluebell) [a]
Phlox spp. and cvs [p]
Primula veris (cowslip) [p]
Quercus spp. and cvs (oak) [t]

Salvia officinalis (sage) [s]
Sambucus niger (black elder) [t]
Sedum spectabile (ice plant) [p]
Thymus spp. and cvs (thyme) [e, s]
Trifolium spp. (wild clover) [p]

Herbs for the kitchen garden
Allium schoenoprasum (chives) [b]
Anethum graveolens (dill) [a]
Borago officinalis (borage) [a]
Chamaemelum nobile (chamomile) [p]
Foeniculum vulgare (fennel) [p]
Laurus nobilis (sweet bay) [e, t]
Mentha spp. and cvs (mint) [p]
Ocimum basilicum (basil) [a]
Origanum spp. and cvs (oregano, marjoram) [p]
Petroselinum spp. and cvs (parsley) [a]
Rosmarinus officinalis (rosemary) [s]
Salvia ssp. and cvs (sage) [s]
Thymus spp. and cvs (thyme) [e, p]

Vegetables, salad, and fruit
apple (*Malus domestica*)
apricot (*Prunus armeniaca*)
asparagus (*Asparagus officinalis*)
beans, broad (*Vicia faba*)
blackberry (*Rubus fruticosus*)
broccoli (*Brassica oleracea*)
carrot (*Daucus carota*)
chard, red-stemmed (*Beta vulgaris* 'Rhubarb Chard')
cherry (*Prunus cerasus* 'Morello')
cucumber (*Cucumis sativus*)
endive, frilly leaved (*Chicorium endivia*)
fig (*Ficus carica*)
gage (*Prunus domestica*)
gooseberry (*Ribes uva-crispa*)
lettuce (*Lactuca sativa*)
mangetout (*Pisum sativum*)
nectarine (*Prunus persica* var. *nectarina*)
onion (*Allium cepa*)
pea (*Pisum sativum*)
peach (*Prunus persica*)
pear (*Pyrus communis* var. *sativa*)
plum (*Prunus domestica*)
potato (*Solanum tuberosum*)
pumpkin (*Curcubita* spp.)
radish (*Raphanus sativus*)
raspberry (*Rubus idaeus*)
spring onion (*Allium cepa* cvs)
strawberry (*Fragaria* x *ananassa*)
sweet pepper (*Capsicum annuum*)
tomato (*Lycopersicon esculentum*)

Index

Acknowledgments

The publisher would like to thank the team of people involved in creating this book. Special thanks go to Brian Mathew, Janet Swarbrick, Sorcha Hitchcox, and Ingrid Lock for their diligence and speed. Also, many thanks to the photographers listed below for supplying a wonderful selection of images.

PICTURE CREDITS

Copyright images are reproduced by kind permission of the following:

Andrew Lawson p.19 (b); p.39 (t, b); p.48 (br); p.53 (r); p.56 (tl); p.58 (bl, br); p.60 (br); p.80; p.89 (br); p.94; p.98 (l); p.107 (bl); p.108; p.121; p.132 (r); p.157 (tl); p.165 (b); p.193 (tr); p.254 (br); p.265 (r); p.286 (tr); p.287 (bl); p.301 (l); p.361 (tl).

John Feltwell p.134 (br); p.135 (tr); p.144-5 (t); p.149; p.151 (tr); p.156; p.165 (tr); p.219 (b); p.249 (b); p.266 (bl, br); p.291 (r); p.337 (br).

John Hedgecoe p.7 (b); .27 (br); p.29; p.134 (ct); p.139 (b); p.145 (b); p. 153 (bl); p.162 (t, b); p.176-7; p.186 (bl); p.190 (bl); p.198 (tr); p.235 (b); p.240 (t); p.246 ; p.264 (t, b); p.272 (t); p.279 (t); p.296; p.302 (bl); p.311; p.316 (tl); p.319; p.321; p.332 (b); p.335 (tr, b); p.353 (t, b); p.360 (br); p.367 (r); pp.370-1; p.371 (b); p.372 (t, b); p.373; pp.374-5; p.378 (bl); p.380; p.381; p.382 (br); p.384; p.385; p.387 (t); p.393 (tr); p.396; p.405 (br); p.412 (tr).

Clive Nichols Front cover (tr); back cover; p.15 design: Keeyla Meadows; p.22; p.47 (tr) garden: Bourton House, Glos; p.51 (br); pp.52-3 design: Bunny Guinness; p.58 (tl) garden: Old Rectory, Berks; p.59 design Anthony Noel; p.60 (tl) design: Geoff Whitten; p.64 (tl) design: Christian Wright; p.66 garden: Chenies Manor, Bucks; p.69 design: Clive Nichols; p.70 (bl) design: Jane & Clive Nichols; p.74 (bl) design: Anthony Noel; p.81; p.92 (t) design: Clive Nichols; p.103 (t) © Graham Strong; p.106; p.110 design: Suzanne Porter; pp.122-3 design: A. Lennox-Boyd; p.123; p.124 (tl) design: Olivia Clark; p.124 (br); p.125 (br) garden: Hadspen Garden, Somerset; p.141 design: Suzanne Porter; p.147 (tl) garden: Greatham Mill, Hants; p.161 (b); p.163 garden: The Anchorage, Kent; p.170 (t); p.178; p.184 (t) design: A. Lennox-Boyd; p.191 garden: Chenies Manor, Bucks; p.202 garden: Hadspen Garden, Somerset; p.205 (tr) garden: Chenies Manor, Bucks; p.206 (bl); p.210 (l); p.212 (br) garden: Sticky Wicket, Dorset; p.216 garden: Chenies Manor, Bucks; p.218 (t) garden: Chenies Manor, Bucks; p.232 design: Olivia Clarke; p.236 design: Olivia Clark; p.237 (t) design: Lisette Pleasance; p.239 (b); p.240 (b); p.241 design: Mr Fraser/J.Treyer-Evans; p.244 (c) design: Anthony Noel; p.247 (bl) design: Anthony Noel; p.252 (br) design: Olivia Clarke; p.258 (tl) design: Nicholas Roeber; p.261 (tl) design: Keeyla Meadows; p.262 (tl); p.267 garden: Vale End, Surrey; p.294 (b) garden: The Old Vicarage, Norfolk; p.295 garden: Hadspen Garden, Somerset; p.305; p.307 (b) garden: Chenies Manor, Bucks; p.312 garden: Eastgrove Cottage, Worcs; p.316 (bl)

garden: Copton Ash, Kent; p.320 (l) garden: Beth Chatto Garden, Essex; p.339; p.343 garden: The Old Vicarage, Norfolk; p.359 (b) design: Mr Fraser/J. Treyer-Evans, p.362 (l) design: Ann Frith, (r) design: Christian Wright; p.365 design: Lucy Smith; p.378-9 (c) garden: Turn End Garden, Bucks; p.383 (t) design: Claus Scheinert; p.387 (cl, cr); p.409; pp.410-1 design: HMP Leyhill; p.426 (tl) design: HMP Leyhill.

Howard Rice pp.174-5; p.228; p.231; p.313; p.317; p.322 (tl); p.324; p.329.

Steve Wooster Front cover (tl, cl, cr, bl); back flap; p.2; pp.6-7; p.9; p.10 (l, r); p.11; p.12; p.13; p.14 (r); pp.18-19; p.20 (tl); p.23 (br) design: Annie Wilkes; p.24 (t, b); p.25; p.26; p.28; p.30; pp.32-3; p.34; p.35 (bl); p.36; p.38 (t) design: Dan Pearson; pp.42-3; p.45 (tr); p.48 (tl); p.49; p.50; p.55 (br); p.57; p.61; p.63 (tr); p.64 (bl); p.65; p.67 (tr); p.68 (l); p.71 (r) design: Paul Cooper; p.75 design: Bunny Guinness/Wye Vale; p.76; p.77 (tl); pp.78-9; p.83 (br); p.84 (l); p.87; p.88; p.90 (tr); p.91 design: Liz Morrow; pp.100-1; p.102 (t, b); p.107 (cr); p.111; p.112; p.114 (t); p.116 design: Anthony Noel; p.117 (br); pp.118-9; p.125 (t); p.126 (tl); p.127; p.129; p.131 (bl); p.133; p.134 (l); p.137; p.138; p.142-3; p.146; p.152; p.153 (cr); p.158; p.160-1; p.164 (br); p.167; p.168; p.173; p.180; p.183; p.189 (t); p.194-5; p.196 (tr); p.199; p.200 (l); p.207 (tr); p.209; p.213; p.214 (l); p.217 (bl); p.220 (bl); p.221; p.222 (l); p.225; pp.226-7; p.230 (tl); p.230 (br) design: Anthony Noel; p.233; p.234 design: Hailstone Landscaping; p.235 (t); p.238 (b); p.239 (t); p.242 design: Henk Weijers; p.243; p.245; p.247 (tr); pp.248-9; p.250; p.251 (bl); p.252 (tl); p.253; p.254 (bl); p.255 design: Anthony Noel; p.256 (t); p.257; p.258 (bl); p.259; p.260; p.266 (tl); p.269 (tl, b); pp.270-1; p.273 (t); p.274; p.275 (l, r); p.277; p.280 (t); p.281 (t); p.283; p.284; p.285 (l); p.286 (tl); p .288; p.289 (tr) design: Jan & Brian Oldham; pp.290-1; p.292 (l, r); p.293 (b); p.294 (t); p.297 (l); p.300; p.304; p.309; p.314 (bl); p.315 (tr); p.318; p.323 design: Anthony Noel; p.330-1; p.332 (t); p.333 (b); p.334; p.337 (t); p.338; p.340 (t, b); p.341 (b); p.342 (b); p.344 (tr); p.347; p.349 (tr); pp.350-1; p.352; p.354; p.355; p.356; p.357; p.358 (b); p.360 (tl); p.363; p.364 (tr); p.366 (r); p.368 (t); p.369 (t); p.377; p.382 (t); p.383 (br); p.386; pp.388-9; p.390 design: Anthony Noel; p.391 (bl); p.392; p.393 (bl); p.394 (tl); p.395 (br); p.397; p.398 (tl); p.399 (t); p.400 (tl, bl); p.402-3 (c); p.404; p.406; p.407 (br); p.413; p.415; p.416; p.420 (r); p.424 (tl, r); p.425 (bl); p.427 (b); p.428.

All other photographs are copyright Kiln House Books.

While every effort has been taken to ensure that all pictures have been fully and correctly credited, the publishers would be pleased to hear of any omissions.